AF251963

WORLD POPULATION
POPULATION

Past, Present, & Future

WORLD POPULATION

Past, Present, & Future

Julio A Gonzalo

Manuel Alfonseca

Félix-Fernando Muñoz

Universidad Autónoma de Madrid, Spain

NEW JERSEY · LONDON · SINGAPORE · BEIJING · SHANGHAI · HONG KONG · TAIPEI · CHENNAI · TOKYO

Published by

World Scientific Publishing Co. Pte. Ltd.

5 Toh Tuck Link, Singapore 596224

USA office: 27 Warren Street, Suite 401-402, Hackensack, NJ 07601

UK office: 57 Shelton Street, Covent Garden, London WC2H 9HE

British Library Cataloguing-in-Publication Data
A catalogue record for this book is available from the British Library.

WORLD POPULATION
Past, Present, & Future

ISBN 978-981-3140-99-8

Desk Editor: Jiang Yulin

Typeset by Stallion Press
Email: enquiries@stallionpress.com

FOREWORD[*]

by Anne Morse and Steven Mosher

We often come across people who attempt to justify forced abortion, sterilization, and contraception because "we (that is, human beings) are destroying the planet." They view people as pollution, and argue that it is necessary to violate reproductive rights to protect the planet from the beings who are despoiling it. Yet that logic is intrinsically flawed.

Let us put it this way. Which of these do not belong: nitrous oxide, methane, Homo sapiens, or carbon dioxide? The obvious answer is: "Homo sapiens."

Pregnant women do not produce nitrous oxide. Childbirth does not generate methane. A newborn baby does exhale carbon dioxide, but this is not a "pollutant" at all but a trace gas on which life depends.

Yes, any given infant may grow up to be a notorious polluter, just as he may grow up to, say, recklessly endanger the lives of others by driving drunk. But such behaviors are not foregone conclusions. Unlike nitrous oxide, methane, or carbon dioxide, human beings have free will.

It is simply not true that more people equal more pollution. We have twice as many people living in the United States as we did in

---

[*] With permission of Steven Mosher, President of Population Institute. We reproduce here the opening article of PRI Review, May-June 2015, entitled "A War on Maternity in the Name of Mother Earth" authored by Anne Morse and Steven Mosher.

the early seventies, yet the skies over our major cities are clearer now than they were a half century ago. This is because the internal combustion engines that power our motor vehicles no longer spew out thousands of tons of particulate matter, sulfur dioxide, and other pollutants into the atmosphere as we drive. And this in turn is because we made a conscious decision to switch to cleaner burning fuels and install catalytic converters downstream from our engines.

Pollution is created by particular human behaviors such as the incomplete combustion of fossil fuels or the indiscriminate spraying of harmful pesticides. It can be corrected by altering those same behaviors. Reducing the number of babies born will not solve these and other environmental problems.

No one would suggest that every baby born into a tech-savvy household will indubitably mature into a cyber terrorist. Yet there are those who seem to believe that every baby human born will mature into a waste-creating, polar bear-murdering, earth-destroying eco-terrorist. This is totally unreasonable. To be sure, some infants will grow up to secretly dump raw sewage into fragile estuaries, but many others will start compost piles and grow their own vegetables in backyard gardens.

No one can guarantee that any given infant will grow up to be a good conservationist, any more than anyone can guarantee that any given infant will grow up into a happy well-adjusted adult. Everyone, as we noted above, enjoys free will.

But it is true that —thanks to technological advances, reasonable environmental regulations, and education that emphasizes good stewardship— we have made great strides in recent decades. Very large populations can actually have a much smaller environmental footprint than a much smaller population did a century or two ago. Population control has no part to play in these successes.

Sadly, not everyone has gotten this message. The anti-people types still argue that babies equal pollution. The population control movement continues to receive billions of dollars in funding each year. Women's fertility continues to be attacked in the name of the environment and "sustainable development."

The United Nations Population Fund (UNFPA) continues to cheerlead China's one-child policy, ignoring the forced abortions and forced sterilizations that follow. The UNFPA continues to distribute 40 million doses of Depo-Provera each year to unsuspecting women— despite the fact that this product is so unsafe that the FDA recommends against its use.

India still sterilizes over 4 million women annually under a system of statewide sterilization targets, ignoring the rising death toll of women who have died in such campaigns. And the developed nations—chief among them the United States—still continue to fund these programs in the name of achieving a mythical "sustainable population," all the while ignoring the massive human rights abuses that they entail.

We agree that pollution sometimes constitutes an offense against other humans beings. Those who wantonly and grossly pollute the water we drink and the air that we breathe endanger the rest of us, both those who are alive now and those who will come later.

But we also insist that forced abortion, forced sterilization, and forced contraception always constitutes a grave violation of human rights. These actions are never justified, least of all by irrationally claiming that they are necessary to "protect the environment."

We look forward to a future where our children and grandchildren enjoy a planet with clean air, clean water, and luxuriant greenery. We have already, in the U.S. and elsewhere, made great strides towards the realization of this future.

But we also hope and pray that our children and grandchildren grow up in a world without population control. The day when they are valued for themselves, and are not seen by many in the environmental movement as a threat to their dream of a world without people.

After all, as Shakespeare remarked, "The world must be peopled".

CONTENTS

SECTION 1

POPULATION, THE ECONOMY, AND THE ENVIRONMENT

Chapter 1
Introductory Considerations
by Julio A. Gonzalo

The 20th century has seen two World Wars, an early scientific revolution, propelled by the birth and development of quantum physics and relativity, and a tremendous technological and industrial revolution in its second half, accompanied by a large growth in world population, which seems to be levelling out in the 21th century, and shows signs of decreasing in the relatively near future.

Scientific discoveries, such as nuclear energy, the solid state transistor, the laser, the structure of DNA (among many others) resulted in revolutionary technological applications, such as computers, space satellites, the great revolution in agriculture, advanced medicine, etc.

The protracted conflict –Cold War– between Soviet Communism and the Free World (lead by the U. S. of America), ended in 1989 with the fall of the Berlin Wall. But local conflicts, all over the world, including the Middle East, Central and South Africa, Central America, and most recently the Mediterranean, go on unabated, as the years go by.

The future of world population is something very difficult (if not impossible) to predict. Together with economic factors –such as energy consumption and food supply–, cultural and spiritual factors are also at play. For instance, the marked decrease in population at the end of the Roman Empire was not due to food scarcity, but rather to moral decay. Short term demographic trends however can be anticipated from the available statistical data.

In this book we examine, in perspective, the recent past, the present and the near future of world population, considering relevant cultural factors and the time evolution of energy consumption.

In Chapter 2, we summarize the unique physiochemical characteristics of our planet, as the only planet in our solar system (and not unlikely in the entire galaxy) capable of housing complex life, most importantly, human life. The Earth is a privileged planet.

Then we examine the UN data for the world population growth in the period 1900-2000, as well as the UN projections up to 2050, which already indicate a moderate decrease in population by the middle of the 21th century. We note that the pronounced increase in population which took place from the middle of the 20th century onwards cannot be due to any global increase in the average family size (fertility), it must be attributed to the overall increase in life expectancy, first in the more developed countries of the world, then in the rest. It must be noted also that the growth in world food production was more pronounced than the growth in population all those years.

Next we give the increase in world energy production and consumption in the same period. Since the greatest shear of primary fuel consumption in the second half of the 20th century was crude oil and natural gas (the supply of which cannot be expected to last indefinitely) after the 1973 oil crisis provoked by the Organization of Petroleum Exporting Countries (OPEC), it became clear than a effort to develop others energy sources (like nuclear energy –fission and fusion–, hydroelectric, wind, solar and biomass energy) will be absolutely necessary.

The question: is the Earth overpopulated? is addressed afterwards. The noted American economist Julian Simon (1932-98) challenged Paul Ehrlich (author of the bestselling *The Population Bomb*) to a wager in 1980 over prices of prime matters (metals) a decade later. Ehrlich, Harte and Holdren selected a basket of five metals that they thought would rise in price. Simon won. Along with Simon's response to the question of the world's overpopulation, the well documented work of Colin Clark and Jacqueline Kasun on the subject is summarized.

It is well known that R. Malthus, the British pioneer theoretical economist antecessor of Ch. Darwin, predicted an exponential growth in population (doubling every 25 years) accompanied only by a linear growth in food production. A more realistic approach, using rate equations, to describe the dynamics of world population is shown to describe well the world demographic evolution during the 20th century. This approach is shown also to predict a considerable decrease in world population from the middle of the present century.

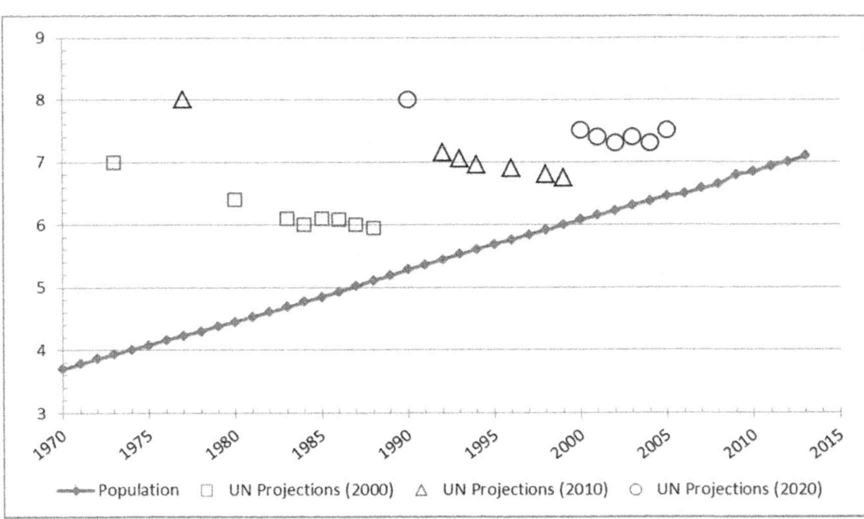

Figure 1.1. UN population projections 2000/2010/2020

The global economic evolution following World War Two; the post-war boom; the collapse of the Bretton Woods system; the 1973 oil crisis and its consequences; the East-Asian boom (first Japan, then China and India); and the economics of energy storage and re-distribution, are all of them briefly analyzed in the perspective of the world population evolution.

It may be noted that the UN demographers did overestimate the expectations of world population growth for the years 2000, 2010 and 2020. In 1974 they estimated a world population of 7.0 billions for the year 2000: actually it was 6.08 billion that year. In 1977 they estimated 8.0 billion for 2010: it came to 6.84. In 1990 they again estimated 8.0 billions for 2020. On the year 2013 it came to 7.09 billion and it should be less than 7.30 billion by 2020, if the present trend continues.

In the final section, recent published works by the authors using the rate equations approach are put together.

CHAPTER 2
THE EARTH AS A PRIVILEGED PLANET

by Julio A. Gonzalo

The planet Earth

The Earth is a relatively small planet orbiting the Sun between Venus and Mars, with the right mass and right chemical composition at the right distance to have developed a "biosphere," with abundant water, and everything else necessary to house *life* in it: unicellular organisms, plants, animals and human beings.

The Sun is an average sized star among the many billions (about 10^{12}) stars in our galaxy, the Milky Way, which occupies the right position (far from the center and not too close to any of the densely populated arms of the galaxy) to avoid the strong radiation background prevalent elsewhere. Its mass insures for the Sun enough fuel (hydrogen and helium) to be radiating sufficient energy for a long period (counted in billion years) but not too much as would be the case with much more massive stars (too short lived).

The Milky Way, in turn, is an average galaxy among the billion galaxies in the observable universe which populate the expanding cosmic sphere, whose radius, according to precise determination made by NASA's satellite WMAP in 2003, is of the order of 46.5 x 10^9 light years, the distance travelled by light since the time of "decoupling" (atom formation, shortly after the Big Bang[1]), to present.

The Earth has an age of the order of 4.6×10^9 years. It is estimated that conditions at the Earth's surface had become favourable for life 4.0×10^9 years ago. The first traces of unicellular life in it have been detected in fossils about 3.8×10^9 years old. As an aside, it may be pointed out that elementary probabilistic considerations, which take into account that all life on Earth is made up of the same twenty left handed amino acids (never their right handed equivalents), make it somewhat difficult to believe for some of us a satisfactory explanation for the origin of life on Earth as *purely* a *chaotic* phenomenon. Any organic synthesis of an amino acid in the laboratory from its chemical components results invariably in 50% left handed and 50% right handed end products.

That the Earth has a spherical shape was something known from the most remote antiquity by the Greeks. Aristotle gives several convincing reasons to prove it. Saint Augustine, eight centuries later, knew them well, and pointed out that when the Bible states something contrary to well established facts, as when the author of the book of Samuel (I Sam. 2) talks of a flat Earth supported on pillars, one must interpret the statement in a proper perspective: the Bible tell us "how to go to Heaven," not "how the Heavens go (or, for that matter, the Earth)."

The Earth's radius, already estimated with surprising precision by Eratosthenes (measuring the arc along the Nile river between Syena (Aswan) and Alexandria) is

$$R_T = 6.378 \text{ km},$$

a very small fraction (less than two per percent) of the distance to the Moon, a minuscule fraction (4.2×10^{-5}) of the distance to the Sun. Taking into account that the Moon covers almost exactly the Sun in a solar eclipse, the large size of the Sun in comparison with that of the Moon (smaller than comparable itself to that of the Earth) becomes evident.

As noted already by Newton, due to the rotation around its axis, the Earth is slightly flattened at the Poles and slightly extended at the Equator. Two thirds of the Earth's surface are covered by water.

In spite of the apparent rugosity of the surface, the deviations from sphericity are in fact very small. The maximum height (mount Everest) is only 0.064 percent of the mean radius, and the depth of the deepest ditch (near the Marianas in the Pacific) is only 0.096 percent.

The Earth–Moon system

The fact that the Moon is a very large satellite, large enough to justify the expression Earth-Moon System, has several important consequences[2]. In the first place it stabilizes the rotation of the Earth, resulting in a more stable, and therefore life-friendly climate. The tilt angle between the Earth's rotation axis and the perpendicular to the plane of its orbit around the Sun, 23.5 degrees plus/minus roughly one degree, is possible because of the relatively large mass of the Moon. A smaller satellite, like Phobos or Deimos would give rise to large variations in the tilt angle, from 30 to 60 degrees, resulting in very large temperature fluctuations, instead of the mild cyclic succession of the four seasons, which, through the regular patterns of the winds and ocean currents, contributes to moderate the temperature difference between extremely hot and extremely cold regions in the terrestrial globe.

On the other hand if the tilt were too small, it would prevent the wide distribution of rains, so necessary for life, on land areas. A planet with little tilt would probably have large extensions of arid land.

The moon also contributes to favour life by rising periodically ocean *tides*. The surface of the rotating Earth facing the Moon experiences a gravitational attraction, which produces periodic displacements of massive amounts of ocean or sea water towards the

Moon. The relation of the Moon tidal[3] acceleration (a_{tide}) to the surface Earth gravitation (g) is given by

$$\frac{a_{tide}}{g} = \frac{2GM_M r_E r^{-3}}{GM_E r_E^{-2}} \cong 2\left(\frac{M_M}{M_E}\right)\left(\frac{r_E}{r}\right)^3 \cong 10^{-7},$$

where G is Newton's gravitational constant G = 6.67×10^{-8} cgs units, M_E= 5.98×10^{27} g the Earth's mass, M_M = 0.73×10^{26} g the Moon's mass, r_E = R_T = 6.37×10^8 cm the Earth's mass, and r is distance of the order of the Earth-Moon distance d = 384×10^8 cm (all in cgs units).

The tidal acceleration is therefore only a small fraction of the Earth gravitational acceleration, but is large enough to displace large amounts of ocean and sea water which can be used as a source of mechanical potential energy, convertible into electrical energy. The strong ocean currents due to the tidal motion produced by the Moon, in combination with that due to the Sun, regulate the Earth's climate by redistributing enormous amounts of heat which are stored continuously in the world oceans. The hurricanes originated in the gulf of Guinea, which move through the Atlantic and visit periodically the Caribbean (Puerto Rico, Santo Domingo, Cuba) and Florida, are good instances of such heat redistribution. Perhaps large scale future engineering projects will take advantage of these enormous amounts of stored heat for some kind of conversion into electrical energy.

The Moon's origin, in a glancing collision[4] of the proto-Earth with a large body a few times more massive than Mars, may have triggered cataclysmic developments such as changing the composition of the Earth's surface, preparing it to become hospitable to life. It may have melted the planet, allowing liquid iron to sink to the center, resulting in a strong planetary magnetic field, instrumental in the formation of the Van Allen belt, which protects life on the

Earth surface. In this way, the collision might have removed material from the Earth crust which could have otherwise prevented plate tectonics, an essential ingredient to a habitable Earth, whith a hydrosphere and atmosphere hospitable to life.

Habitability

Habitability depends drastically on the size of the planet, its accompanying satellites, and the host star, as well as on the separation between them. Besides, the protecting role of large bodies orbiting further away in the same plane cannot be neglected.

The geological history, sustaining atmosphere and protective magnetic field play also essential roles.

The present internal structure of the Earth has been determined by means of measurements of the propagation speed of shock waves resulting from the earthquakes. Under the external *crust*, with density between $1 g/cm^3$ (water) and $2.7 g/cm^3$ (land), is the *mantle*, made up of metallic oxides (perovskites and other oxides), with densities around $3.3 g/cm^3$, and down deeper, the central *core*, made up of iron and nickel, subject to high pressures and high temperatures. These high temperatures are in good measure due to the heat liberated by the emissions of radioactive isotopes.

The mean density of the Earth is $5.5 g/cm^3$, much higher than that of the surface layer which makes up the continental lands and the oceans. The stability of large mountainous masses, like the Himalaya or the Andes, implies that, behind them, there are large masses of the same density, so to say, "floating" (*isostasis*) on the surface layer of the crust, which has a larger average density.

The atmosphere

The terrestrial atmosphere is made of a gaseous mixture of *nitrogen, oxygen* and lesser amounts of carbon dioxide (CO_2), water vapour (H_2O) and some noble gases. The density of air in normal conditions (0 °C of temperature 760 mm of Hg at the seaside) is 1.3 $\times$ 10^{-3} g/cm^3, intermediate between that of molecular nitrogen and molecular oxygen under the same conditions. Of course, as one rises higher over the Earth surface, the air density decreases and, above one to two hundred kilometres, the density becomes progressively very small. Because of that the meteorites and foreign bodies which approach the Earth from outer space become visible at heights of that order above the surface. Commercial jets, as it is well known, fly about ten kilometers above the Earth's surface, where the air density is still substantial.

Atmospheric temperature and pressure depend on the influx of solar radiation, on the location (longitude and latitude) and on the proximity or not of water or land areas. The local fluctuations of density and temperature and the humidity of the air gives rise to winds, rains, tempests and spectacular hurricanes and monsoons, in which air currents have become overheated in contact with warm surface water, and torrential rains are violently discharged when arriving to land areas. The energy which is liberated in some of these natural phenomena is much larger than that discharged in a typical atomic bomb explosion, and the effects may be truly devastating.

In general, the atmosphere acts as an effective insulator, avoiding violent changes in temperature between extreme heat and glacial cold, between day and night, such as those which take place, for instance, in Mars, a relatively close planet. In the Moon, closest to Earth, with no atmosphere, and in Venus and Mars, with some kind of atmosphere, very different to the Earth's, there is no life. The philosophers of the Enlightenment, in the seventeenth century, and later (Diderot, D'Alembert, Kant, Hegel, etc.), were all convinced that intelligent inhabitants were populating all solar planets. Even recently the NASA space missions to Mars expected to find abundant evidence of life there. But the general disappointment in not finding life was soon forgotten.

Only the Earth, the "Blue Planet," meets all the strict requirements to house life, not to say *intelligent life*, within its confines. Kant took for granted that the inhabitants of Mars, cooler than Earth, must be much more intelligent than we, inhabitants of a relatively warm Earth.

The oldest and primitive civilizations took advantage of agriculture, cattle and livestock. They produced ceramics out of heated up clay, and begun to use metals scarcely 10,000 years ago. The beautifully painted scenes of hunting in Altamira and Lascaux are only 30,000 to 40,000 years old. The last glaciations took place about 60,000 years. There is no conclusive evidence that the older paleontological remains found in various places can be properly ascribed to rational men (*homo sapiens*).

Preconditions for life on Earth

Michael Denton[5] has made up a list of preconditions for life, which is, by no means, exhaustive. All of them are met today in our planet and for the moment, there is no clear evidence that they are met in any other planet surrounding a Sun-like star within our galaxy. Some of these preconditions are general cosmic preconditions, necessary for the existence of the nuclei of the atoms in the periodic table, for the existence of stable atomavenues of further discovery on the subject ofs and molecules, themselves in a certain range of temperatures, and also for the existence of long lived stars and planets. Some others are more specific preconditions for the necessary existence on the Earth of certain atomic species, with special physicochemical characteristics, and of some happy coincidences in the masses and locations of the planetary system in which the "privileged" planet, capable of sustaining complex life, is placed. A somewhat modified version of the list includes:

1) *The* primordial nucleosynthesis *of ^4He in the right proportion, at temperatures of the order of $T \cong 4.6 \times 10^8 K$, which resulted in the proper ratio of neutrons to protons and protons to electrons in the hot plasma universe previous to decoupling and atom formation.*

2) *The occurrence of* stable *atoms at temperatures under the temperature of ionization of the hydrogen atom (about 4×10^3 K).*

3) *The existence of light, intermediate and massive* isotopes *produced in the interior of early stars, burned up prior to the formation of the Sun (a star of second or third generation) out of cosmic dust due to those early massive stars.*

4) *The stability of the nuclei of* light elements *such as C, O, N, S absolutely* indispensable *for life, and their abundance on the surface on the Earth-like planet in question. In particular, the absolutely unique chemical properties of the carbon atom (C).*

5) *The stability and relative abundance of nuclei of* heavier elements *such as Mg, Ca, Sr, Ba, etc. to constitute the* crust *and the* mantle, *as well as the stability and relative abundance of nuclei of transition elements, Fe, Ni, Co, capable to constituting the* magnetic core *for the planet in question. Mg is essential to chlorophyll (photosynthesis) and Fe is essential to haemoglobin (respiration).*

6) *That the respective masses and the distance between the* planet *in question and the* host stars *be within narrow*

limits (not too near, not too far), so that the surface temperature of the planet is around 300° K, intermediate between the melting and vaporization points of water, so that H2O can exist comfortably on the planet's surface in the solid, liquid and gaseous states.

7) *The existence of a* central hot core *in the planet, due at least in part, to radioactive nuclei disintegration, sufficient to produce* plate tectonics, *contributing to the essential "oxygen cycle," the "carbon cycle" and the "nitrogen cycle" in the planet. This accompanied by a prolonged bombardment by water and CO2 containing asteroids, meteorites and comets, during a sufficiently long early period.*

8) *That the mass of the planet in question be sufficient to hold in place an* atmosphere *rich in O2 and N2.*

9) *That it has a* large satellite *capable of stabilizing the tilt of its rotation axis so as to avoid very extreme temperatures, and to insure a succession of well-timed day/night sequence, combined with a mild succession of the four stations: spring-summer-autumn-winter.*

10) *That the planet in question must have also a* large planetary companion *(of Jupiter size) capable of protecting it from the excessive bombardment of heavy asteroids and meteorites.*

11) *The presence in the high atmosphere (*ionosphere*) of abundant circulating ions, held in place by the planet's magnetic field, producing some kind of protective* Van Allen belt *to reduce substantially the incoming cosmic radiation. (If the planetary system housing the planet in question were located near the galaxy center, any Van Allen belt protection would be utterly insufficient).*

12) *Foremost: the existence in the planet's surface of* abundant water, *with the exceptional chemical properties of*

the water molecule, which make it absolutely indispensable for life.

13) Equally important: the existence in the planet's surface of abundant carbon *(also with exceptional chemical properties) and carbon containing molecules (for instance CO_2), which make possible photosynthesis, taking advantage of the solar radiation to synthesize organic matter.*

14) Finally, the unique biochemical properties of nucleic acids (DNA and RNA) which, in tandem with the proteins, make possible the tremendous diversity and complexity of life in the vegetal and animal kingdoms.

It would not be difficult to add many more preconditions for life, but the ones enumerated make it clear that the existence of life on Earth is not a trivial random fact to be expected beforehand, even in a system as vast as our galaxy.

Life's origin, life's stability and the development of the complex life tree in our privileged planet may be natural developments, but they are not random.

The "trousered" ape

Definitely non-random is the emergence on Earth of the most anomalous species to walk on it: the *trousered ape*, to use a felicitous expression by C. S. Lewis.

Man is the only ape capable of smiling, of looking at the stars (and among myriads, the Polar Star), of speaking in a thousand tongues, and writing in a hundred alphabets, of playing a hundred games, including football, poker and chess, producing movies, and organizing Olympic games…

The only ape who has constructed massive Egyptian Pyramids, great Chinese Walls, and beautiful Cathedrals in Medieval Catholic Europe.

The only one who has made history, science and poetry. The only ape capable of appreciating good, truth and beauty, evil, imposture and ugliness.

The only ape who has been able to make computers, supersonic jets and nuclear reactors.

The only ape who did fly to the Moon.

An ape capable of doing much good and much evil, because he was created free.

Evidently there is a tremendous discontinuity between the orangutan, the gorilla and the chimpanzee, which appeared on our planet fifteen, ten, five million years ago, and man (with or without trousers), who, within the short period of about twenty five thousand years, has gone from painting the beautiful primitive paintings of Altamira and Lascaux, to painting the Sistine Chapel.

Paraphrasing Chesterton, many years ago, a primitive man could have painted a primitive gorilla, but nobody expects to find today remnants of the portrait of a primitive man painted by a primitive gorilla.

Some trousered apes today, including many Darwinist professors, insist in putting themselves in a par with orangutans, gorillas and chimps. They feel superior to their fathers and grandfathers because they have come to the wrong conclusion that God is *not* needed and everything in Nature are random ocurrences.

No way: a mere one percent difference between the genome of a chimpanzee and the genome of a man does not explain the difference between what chimps and men have achieved in thirty five thousand years.

Of course human beings share many things in common with the higher animals. They have instincts. But we have been created by God with an immortal soul.

This explains the *tremendous discontinuity* between the "trousered" ape and the rest.

God is obviously needed, not only to create the universe, life, and the "trousered" ape, but to keep the whole universe (life, apes and men) in existence.

REFERENCES

[1] Julio A. Gonzalo, "Inflationary Cosmology Revisited" (*World Scientific*: Singapore, 2005).

[2] Guillermo González and Jay W. Richards, "The Privileged Planet" (*Regnery Publishing, Inc*: Washington, 2004), pp. 4-6.

[3] See, for instance, Gerthsen-Kneser-Vogel, *Física* (Springer Verlag, Editorial Dossat S.A.: Madrid, 1977).

[4] Guillermo González and Jay W. Richards, *Ibidem*, p. 6, note 11.

[5] Michael Denton, *Evolution: A Theory in Crisis* (Adler and Adler: Bethesda, Maryland, 1985), chap. 11.

CHAPTER 3
MATHEMATICAL DESCRIPTIONS OF POPULATION TRENDS[*]

by Julio A. Gonzalo and Manuel Alfonseca

In this chapter we have selected six of the main milestones in the field of population dynamics, namely: Edmond Halley, Leonhard Euler, Thomas Robert Malthus, Pierre François Verhulst, the Club of Rome and Robert McCredie May, following mainly a recent historical book (Bakaër 2011), which we have completed with a short description of our own work in the area.

Edmond Halley (1656-1742)

Around 1690, Caspar Neumann collected data in Breslau (Wroclaw) about the number of births and deaths in his city and the age of people at death. Neumann sent his data to Henry Justel (secretary of the Royal Society). Halley got hold of the data, analyzed them, noticed that the population, the number of births and the number of deaths remained constant in those five years (1687-1691) and built a life table showing the population in the city as a function of age. His formula was simple: given that P_0 = population with 0 years of age must be equal to the number of births in the year (a mean of

---

[*] J. A. Gonzalo, Manuel Alfonseca, *Mathematical Description of World Population Trends*, Journal of Global Issues and Solutions, January-February 2016 Issue

1238), the population at age k+1 must be:

$$P_{k+1} = P_k - D_k \tag{1}$$

where D_k is the number of deaths in the year at age k. Adding all the elements in the table, Halley got an estimate of the total population of Breslau (which had not been stated in Neumann's data) as about 34,000. Halley then used the data to build a table to compute the price of life annuities, although his results (which were reasonable) were never taken into account in practice. This table was built starting from the fact that the probability that a person who is alive at age k be still alive at age k+n would be $\frac{P_{k+n}}{P_k}$, which could be computed from his life table.

Leonhard Euler (1707-1783)

The famous Swiss mathematician Euler was also one of the pioneers of mathematical demography. Rather than tackling a stable population, as Halley had done, Euler considered the situation where a population grows at a constant rate x. As the situation is exactly the same as that in compound interest, the formula he reached was:

$$P_n = (1 + x)^n P_0 \tag{2}$$

where P_0 is the initial population and n is the number of years. This formula corresponds to a geometric progression, also called an exponential growth.

In a later work (*A general investigation into the mortality and multiplication of the human species*), published in 1760 in the Proceedings of the Academy of Sciences in Berlin, he analyzed the following situation:

A population in exponential growth: $P_n = r^n P_0$

The birth rate is constant: $m = B_n / P_n$. Therefore $B_n = r^n B_0$.

The death rate is constant, ergo $D_n = r^n D_0$. From here we get:

$$m = \frac{1-r}{\frac{D_n}{B_n} - r}. \text{ Also, } r = \frac{P_n - D_n}{P_n - B_n}.$$

Let $P_{k,n}$ be the population at the beginning of year n with an age k. The survival coefficient q_k (the proportion of the population that reach age k) is: $q_k = P_{k,n} / P_{0,n-k}$. These coefficients can also be computed thus: $q_{k+1} = q_k - \frac{r^k D_{k,n}}{B_n}$, where $D_{k,n}$ is the number of deaths at age k during the year n. The initial coefficient is $q_0 = 1$.

The maximum age reached by a member of the population is 100 years.

From these assumptions, Euler derived his demographic equation, namely:

$$1 = m \left(1 + \frac{q_1}{r} + \frac{q_2}{r^2} + \ldots + \frac{q_{100}}{r^{100}}\right) \tag{3}$$

which is the same as Halley's equation when r=1.

Although Euler was the first to prove that in a population in exponential growth the shape of the age pyramid remains constant, this discovery was not taken into account until it was rediscovered in the twentieth century. Of course, assuming an exponential growth for extended periods would be an unrealistic assumption.

Thomas Robert Malthus (1766-1834)

In 1798, Malthus published (anonymously) a book entitled *An essay on the principle of population, as it affects the future improvement of society, with remarks on the speculations of Mr. Godwin, M. Condorcet, and other writers*. This book includes the famous quotation:

> *Assuming then my postulata as granted, I say, that the power of population is indefinitely greater than the power in the earth to produce subsistence for man.*

> *Population, when unchecked, increases in a geometrical ratio. Subsistence increases only in an arithmetical ratio. A slight acquaintance with numbers will shew the immensity of the first power in comparison of the second.*

In other words, population grows exponentially (or in a geometric progression) as Euler had assumed, but food production grows in an arithmetic progression, i.e. linearly. Therefore, the geometric increase of the population must be stopped by the effects of famine.

Malthus made two mistakes:

1. Extending the exponential growth of population indefinitely. As Gordon Moore expressed it in a meeting of the IBM Academy in 2003: *No exponential is forever*.

2. Assuming that food production cannot grow exponentially. However, the agricultural revolution of the nineteenth and twentieth century produced exactly that result.

Charles Darwin and Alfred Russell Wallace applied (and cited) the ideas of Malthus to develop the theory of evolution by means of natural selection.

Pierre François Verhulst (1804-1849)

In 1838, as a reaction against Malthus theory, the Belgian Verhulst proposed (in his *Note on the law of population growth*) the following equation to represent the growth of population:

$$\frac{dP}{dt} = rP \left(1 - \frac{P}{K}\right) \tag{4}$$

This is the *logistic equation*. Parameter K is arbitrary. If its value is infinite, we get exponential growth. If it is finite, the solution to this equation resembles exponential growth up to an inflection point (at a value of P=K/2) and then becomes convex upwards and grows ever more slowly until it reaches (at time infinite) the value K. Figure 3.1 shows the *logistic curve*.

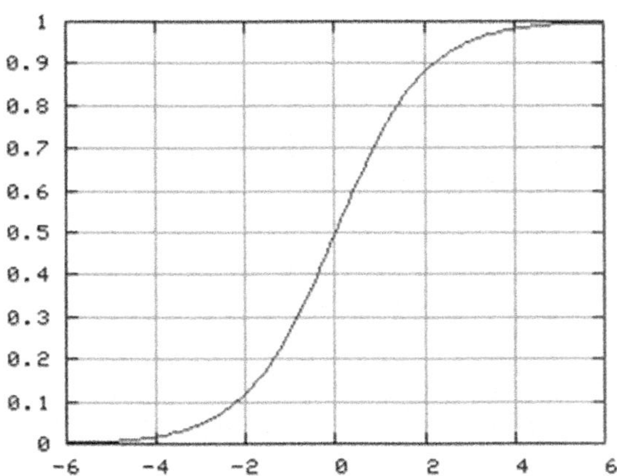

Figure 3.1. The logistic curve for K=1

Verhulst tested the logistic curve against real data from France,

Belgium and the U.S.A. and got a good fit. However, his predictions for longer times (around 50 years) did not come true. The problem in his case is that the two parameters in his equation (the growth rate r and the limiting value K) are not really constant, but time dependent. With an appropriate technology that increases the resources of the world along time, the value of K can be increased above its value around the mid-nineteenth century.

Club of Rome (1968-)

In 1972, the Club of Rome published its first report, the best-selling book *The limits to growth*, which described a model based on five variables: world population, pollution, industrialization, food production and resources depletion. Following Malthus, these five variables are assumed to grow exponentially, while the resource growth as a consequence of technological advances was supposed to be only linear. The model consisted of about 1000 equations, and the authors studied three different future scenarios, two of which would lead to the collapse of human civilization, while the third (of course, favored) would lead to stabilization. The book has been considered too pessimistic and its growth assumptions arbitrary. In fact, world population growth has been observed to go through the inflection point in the logistic curve around 1985, which means that this growth is no longer exponential.

In 1974, the second report of the Club of Rome (*Mankind at the turning point*) presented a more complicated model (about 200,000 equations), integrating, not just technological, but also social data, which lead to more optimistic predictions, signaling that many of the future factors are under the control of mankind and therefore may be changed.

The reports of the Club of Rome have been checked with real data in the forty years passed since their publication, the reviewers sorting themselves among those who assert that the predictions of the Club are being confirmed, and those who claim that they have been proved incorrect.

Robert McCredie May (1936-)

In 1974, the Australian born Robert May published in *Science* an important paper addressing the problem of computing the population dynamics when the resources of the environment are limited (in other words, when the population size cannot go much higher than a certain maximum K). The model he proposed was a discrete equivalent of Verhulst logistic equation:

$$p_{n+1} = p_n + ap_n \left(1 - \frac{p_n}{K}\right) \tag{5}$$

This equation works for $0<a\leq3$. Figure 3.2 shows the solutions for the equation for several values of parameter a, and for K=1000.

It can be seen (and proved mathematically) that for a<2, the equation converges to a single value; for $2\leq a<2.45$, it converges to a period 2 cycle; for $2.45\leq a<2.545$, it converges to a period 4 cycle; and for $2.57\leq a\leq3$, the equation becomes chaotic. Populations, therefore, can be subject to quite unpredictable dynamics, which makes it possible that the optimistic or pessimistic predictions by different authors may not be according to reality.

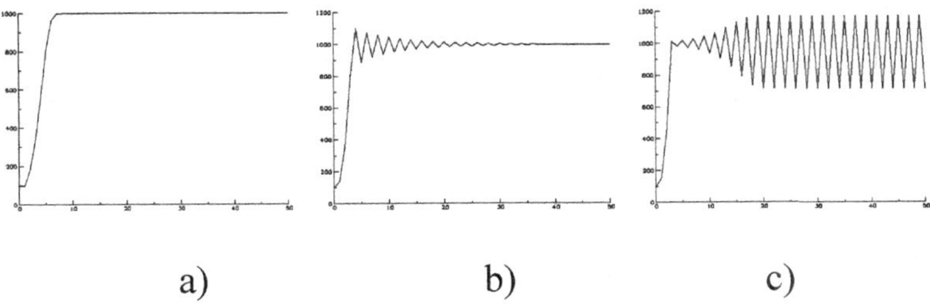

a)   b)   c)

Figure 3.2. Solutions for May equation. a) a=1; b) a=1.9; c) a=2.25; d) a=2.5; e) a=3

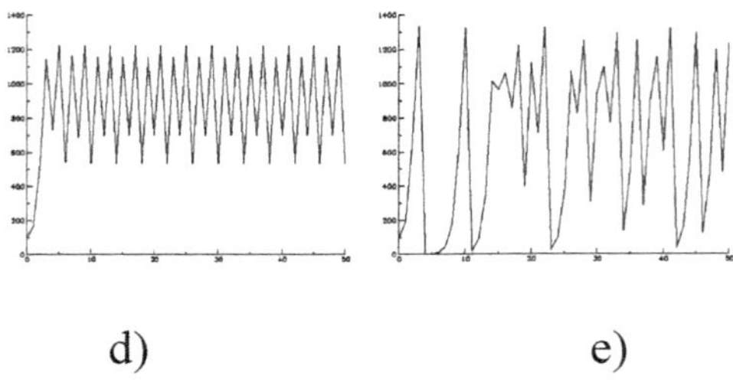

d)   e)

Figure 3.2. (Cont'd)

Equation (5) can be simplified to (6) by means of the following variable changes:

$$r = a + 1 \qquad x_n = \frac{ap_n}{K(a + 1)}$$

$$x_{n+1} = rx_n (1 - x_n) \tag{6}$$

Julio A. Gonzalo *et al*

Using UN population data for the interval 1900-2010, we have simulated its time evolution by means of rate equations inspired on condensed matter physics (Gonzalo et al 2012). The final differential equation to be solved was:

$$\frac{dp(t)}{dt} = \frac{1}{\tau}[\sinh \alpha - p(t) \cosh \alpha] \tag{7}$$

whose solution is:

$$P(t) = P_{RL} + \Delta P_{max}\tan\alpha\left[1 - e^{-\frac{t-t_i}{\tau^*}}\right] \tag{8}$$

where $\tau^* = \tau / \cosh\alpha$.

Equation (8) describes a step up in population due to an increase in fertility rate, a decrease in death rate (life expectancy increase) or a combination of both, resulting in a net growth rate. This equation fits the UN data satisfactorily and shows clearly that the population increase in 1950–2010 should be attributed more to the transient decrease in death rate level (related to the increase in life expectancy) than to a non-existent increase in birth rate, which was decreasing consistently already even before the 1950s, even before chemical contraceptives and legalized abortion begun to play any role.

An equivalent approximate form of equation (8) is:

$$P(t) = P_{RL} + \frac{1}{2}\left[\Delta P_{max}\tanh\alpha\right]\left[1 + \tanh\frac{t-t_i}{\tau_i}\right] \tag{9}$$

Using this equation we analyzed the three future scenarios estimated from the UN data and came to the following conclusions (Gonzalo et al 2015): Today the world is not overpopulated and is unlikely to be so in the foreseeable future. Extrapolating present trends shows that total world population may reach a maximum of 7.74 billion by 2050, and by the end of the current century it may have decreased. Assuming that the smooth natural decrease in birth rate by the mid-seventies had continued all the way down, the estimated population maximum would have reached 8.4 billion by 2065, rather than 7.74 billion by 2050; therefore the policies aimed at lowering the birth rate supported by the UN should be reconsidered. The population rise during this century (1950-2050) is due to the high and sustained decrease in death rate (and the corresponding high increase in life expectation) rather than an increase in fertility that actually never happened.

REFERENCES

[1] Nicolas Bacaër, 2011. *A short history of mathematical population dynamics*, Springer.
[2] Meadows, D. H.; Meadows, D. L.; Randers, J.; Behrens III, W. W., 1972. *The Limits to Growth: a report for the Club of Rome's project on the predicament of mankind*, Universe Books.
[3] Mesarovic, M.; Pestel, E., 1974. *Mankind at the Turning Point. The Second Report to the Club of Rome*, New York: E.P. Dutton.
[4] Gonzalo, J.A., Muñoz, F.F., Santos, D.J., 2012. *Using a rate equation approach to model world population trends*. Simulation 89(2), 192-198, DOI:10.1177/0037549712463736. Reprinted as chapter 10 in this book.
[5] Muñoz, F.F., Gonzalo, J.A., 2013. *Falling birth rates and world population decline 1950-2040*. Departamento de Análisis Económico, U.A.M.
[6] Gonzalo, J.A., Muñoz, F.F., 2014. *Prospects of world population decline in the near future: a short note*. Departamento de Análisis Económico, U.A.M.
[7] Gonzalo, J.A., Alfonseca, M., 2015. *Quantitative estimates of the future world population decline*. Journal of Global Issues and Solutions, The Bimonthly Journal of the BWW Society, 6 pp. Reprinted as chapter 13 in this book.

CHAPTER 4
WORLD POPULATION GROWTH: 1900-2010: THE UN DATA
by Julio A. Gonzalo and Manuel Alfonseca

Population growth data

First let us take a look at the UN data in Table 4.1[1,2].

Table 4.1. UN data for the population of the world and its main divisions, 1900-2010

Year	Europe	Asia	Africa	N.Amer	L.Amer.	Oceania	World	Incr.	% Incr.
1900	408000	947000	133000	82000	74000	6000	1650000		
1910							1750000	10000	0.61%
1920							1860000	11000	0.63%
1930							2070000	21000	1.13%
1940							2300000	23000	1.11%
1950	549043	1395749	228827	171615	167869	12675	2525779	40000	1.61%
1951	554239	1425762	233364	174093	172397	12996	2572851	47072	1.86%
1952	559756	1454049	238148	176911	177134	13294	2619292	46441	1.81%
1953	565441	1481619	243180	180001	182042	13582	2665865	46573	1.78%
1954	571184	1509265	248460	183299	187092	13871	2713172	47307	1.77%
1955	576912	1537568	253988	186744	192271	14167	2761651	48479	1.79%
1956	582596	1566882	259762	190281	197577	14474	2811572	49921	1.81%
1957	588247	1597347	265780	193855	203022	14792	2863043	51471	1.83%
1958	593907	1628917	272039	197420	208628	15118	2916030	52987	1.85%
1959	599645	1661410	278537	200931	214426	15448	2970396	54366	1.86%

Table 4.1. (Cont'd)

Year	Europe	Asia	Africa	N.Amer	L.Amer.	Oceania	World	Incr.	% Incr.
1960	605517	1694650	285270	204352	220439	15775	3026003	55607	1.87%
1961	611540	1728620	292240	207654	226676	16100	3082830	56827	1.88%
1962	617656	1763602	299448	210820	233121	16424	3141072	58241	1.89%
1963	623724	1800230	306902	213842	239723	16757	3201178	60107	1.91%
1964	629551	1839326	314611	216723	246417	17111	3263739	62561	1.95%
1965	635004	1881423	322581	219467	253153	17494	3329122	65384	2.00%
1966	640021	1926743	330825	222067	259911	17909	3397475	68353	2.05%
1967	644645	1974950	339344	224528	266704	18351	3468522	71046	2.09%
1968	648980	2025319	348133	226881	273557	18805	3541675	73153	2.11%
1969	653184	2076816	357178	229169	280508	19253	3616109	74434	2.10%
1970	657369	2128631	366475	231429	287588	19681	3691173	75064	2.08%
1971	661569	2180608	376024	233672	294797	20084	3766754	75582	2.05%
1972	665747	2232791	385844	235903	302122	20466	3842874	76119	2.02%
1973	669861	2284815	395980	238139	309560	20827	3919182	76309	1.99%
1974	673848	2336301	406489	240395	317104	21168	3995305	76123	1.94%
1975	677662	2387024	417413	242685	324746	21492	4071020	75716	1.90%
1976	681298	2436768	428768	245021	332486	21795	4146136	75115	1.85%
1977	684781	2485677	440551	247408	340319	22081	4220817	74681	1.80%
1978	688129	2534347	452764	249840	348224	22361	4295665	74848	1.77%
1979	691365	2583628	465401	252306	356174	22653	4371528	75863	1.77%
1980	694510	2634161	478459	254800	364150	22968	4449049	77521	1.77%
1981	697550	2685977	491937	257318	372142	23310	4528235	79186	1.78%
1982	700485	2738950	505830	259869	380150	23678	4608962	80728	1.78%
1983	703365	2793364	520125	262463	388177	24066	4691560	82597	1.79%
1984	706254	2849521	534803	265114	396235	24466	4776393	84833	1.81%
1985	709189	2907535	549846	267831	404329	24872	4863602	87209	1.83%
1986	712194	2967577	565244	270624	412455	25284	4953377	89775	1.85%

Table 4.1. (Cont'd)

Year	Europe	Asia	Africa	N.Amer	L.Amer.	Oceania	World	Incr.	% Incr.
1987	715224	3029310	580985	273489	420605	25702	5045316	91939	1.86%
1988	718171	3091691	597043	276406	428780	26125	5138215	92899	1.84%
1989	720883	3153313	613385	279344	436980	26548	5230452	92238	1.80%
1990	723248	3213123	629987	282286	445203	26969	5320817	90364	1.73%
1991	725255	3270765	646850	285209	453442	27388	5408909	88092	1.66%
1992	726928	3326386	663971	288124	461687	27803	5494900	85991	1.59%
1993	728243	3380074	681313	291090	469928	28217	5578865	83966	1.53%
1994	729179	3432105	698832	294185	478152	28633	5661086	82221	1.47%
1995	729743	3482719	716505	297458	486345	29052	5741822	80736	1.43%
1996	729911	3531856	734327	300942	494505	29476	5821017	79194	1.38%
1997	729736	3579497	752336	304597	502618	29905	5898688	77672	1.33%
1998	729396	3625999	770604	308319	510647	30339	5975304	76615	1.30%
1999	729127	3671836	789232	311960	518545	30779	6051478	76174	1.27%
2000	729105	3717372	808304	315417	526278	31224	6127700	76222	1.26%
2001	729384	3762760	827848	318645	533838	31672	6204147	76447	1.25%
2002	729934	3808002	847882	321680	541231	32125	6280854	76707	1.24%
2003	730744	3853120	868465	324601	548468	32593	6357992	77138	1.23%
2004	731770	3898086	889664	327528	555567	33090	6435706	77714	1.22%
2005	732970	3942882	911528	330546	562546	33623	6514095	78389	1.22%
2006	734361	3987509	934079	333681	569400	34198	6593228	79133	1.21%
2007	735929	4032014	957318	336900	576136	34808	6673106	79878	1.21%
2008	737546	4076463	981243	340154	582806	35437	6753649	80543	1.21%
2009	739047	4120930	1005838	343372	589476	36059	6834722	81073	1.20%
2010	740308	4165440	1031084	346501	596191	36659	6916183	81462	1.19%

The data in Table 4.1 are divided into two very different sections:

- From 1900 to 1950 estimations are rough and distant (ten years interval), as data could not be collected in a reliable way.

- From 1950 to 2010 estimations are more reliable and are given in intervals of one year.

The last two columns in Table 4.1 show the yearly increments of world population in absolute value and percentage. To compute the values shown for 1910 to 1940, I have simply divided by ten the 10-year increments. This procedure gives too-small increments for 1950, where the fast increase had already started, predictably around 1945. Therefore I simply put there one intermediate value of 40.000 (forty million people) for the absolute increment, and computed the corresponding percentage. Observe that the fact that ten year intervals are used between 1900 and 1950, the effect of the two world wars on the world population (10 and 50 million deaths each) is hidden, although that effect may have been compensated somewhat by the well-known fact that wars usually give rise to an increase in birth rate.

It can be seen in the last column of the table that the percentage of increase in the world population reached a maximum of just a little above 2% between 1965 and 1972 with a maximum (2.11%) in 1968. Precisely in that year, the Club of Rome was founded to analyze the dangers humanity was facing. In 1972 they publish their report "The limits to growth," which became famous because of its pessimistic overreached predictions. In the case of population growth, they assumed that a yearly increment above 2% would be maintained indefinitely, giving rise to the consequent exponential growth with terrifying consequences. Assuming a yearly growth exactly equal to 2%, an exponential growth would predict about 9 billion people living on the Earth by 2015, 18 billion people by 2050 and about 50 billion by 2100. These predictions have now been proved excessive.

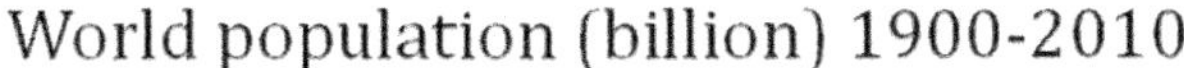

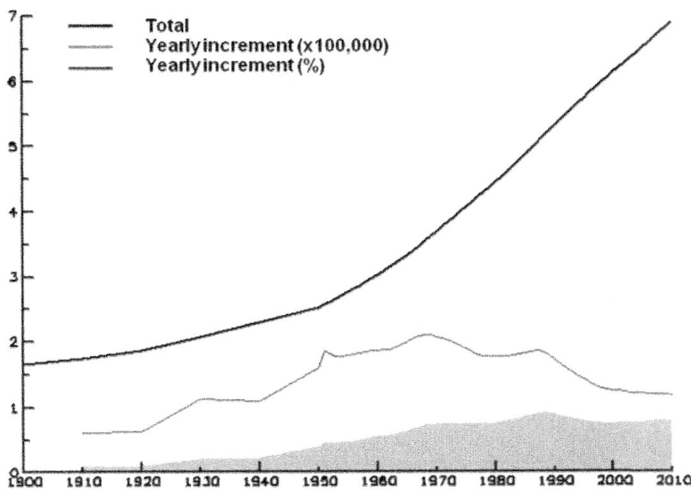

Figure 4.1. UN data for the population of the world (top) and the yearly increment (absolute at bottom and percentage in the middle)

As Gordon Moore said in 2003, in a lecture at the IBM Academia, *no natural growth is exponential forever*. He was actually speaking about his own law, which applies to the growth of the number of components in a computer chip, but what he said is applicable to every other natural growth process. In fact, these processes can be better approximated by a hyperbolic tangent [3] or by the logistic curve. In both cases, the apparent exponential initial growth of the process will sooner or later reach an inflection point, from which point the growth will diminish gradually until a new plateau is reached, when the growth disappears and the process or magnitude stabilizes.

Figure 4.1 shows the world population data in Table 4.1 plus the yearly increase, represented in two ways (absolute and percentage). It can be seen that, from 1968, the percentage increase has gone down significantly to pre-1950 values (1.19 in 2010). At the same time, in 1988 the absolute increase reached a maximum of over 92 million people and then started diminishing, although the global increase of population has given rise to a slow growth of the absolute increase since 1999.

World population (billion) 1950-2010

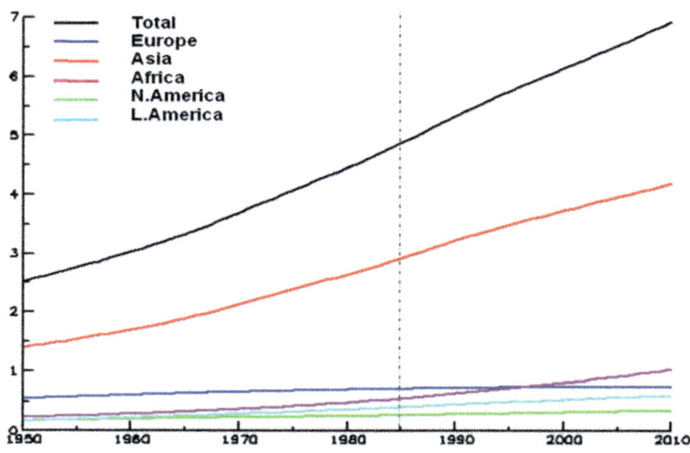

Figure 4.2. UN data for the population of the world (black) and the different parts of the world (colors). The apparent inflection point in the growth is shown at 1985

Figure 4.2 shows the global world population data between 1950 and 2010, together with its distribution in different parts of the world. It can be seen that the inflection point probably took place around 1985 (the global curve is visibly concave to the left of that point and convex to the right), although we are too near the critical point for the effect to be outstanding. It can also be noticed that the population of Europe has already stabilized, while those of the other parts are still growing, although all of them except Africa have already gone through the inflection point. It is precisely the African effect that is slowing the convexity of the global growth.

Birth and death rate data

Tables 4.2 and 4.3 show the UN data in births/deaths per tousand population [4,5]. In this case, the data are accumulated in five-year periods.

Table 4.2. UN data for the birth rate in the world and its main divisions, 1950-2010

Year	Europe	Asia	Africa	N.America	L.America	Oceania	World
1950-55	21,5	42,0	48,1	24,6	42,6	27,4	37,0
1955-60	20,9	39,5	47,9	24,8	41,8	27,3	35,6
1960-65	19,0	39,7	47,4	22,5	41,0	26,2	35,3
1965-70	16,8	37,9	46,4	18,1	37,8	24,5	33,5
1970-75	15,6	34,3	45,9	15,6	35,2	24,1	31,1
1975-80	14,8	29,7	45,5	14,9	33,0	21,0	28,3
1980-85	14,4	28,9	44,4	15,4	30,7	20,4	27,8
1985-90	13,7	28,7	42,6	15,7	27,9	19,8	27,4

Table 4.2. (Cont'd)

Year	Europe	Asia	Africa	N.America	L.America	Oceania	World
1990-95	11,5	24,5	40,4	15,4	25,4	19,6	24,3
1995-00	10,2	21,0	38,8	14,2	23,6	18,7	21,8
2000-05	10,1	19,3	37,7	13,8	21,6	17,8	20,6
2005-10	10,8	18,5	36,7	13,7	19,3	17,8	20,1

Table 4.3. UN data for the death rate in the world and its main divisions, 1950-2010

Year	Europe	Asia	Africa	N.America	L.America	Oceania	World
1950-55	11,2	22,6	26,8	9,5	15,5	12,4	19,1
1955-60	10,2	20,2	24,3	9,3	13,7	11,3	17,3
1960-65	9,7	18,9	22,2	9,3	12,2	10,6	16,2
1965-70	9,9	13,3	20,4	9,4	10,9	10,0	12,9
1970-75	10,2	11,3	18,7	9,2	9,7	9,4	11,6
1975-80	10,5	9,9	17,1	8,6	8,7	8,6	10,6
1980-85	10,8	9,1	15,7	8,5	7,8	8,0	10,0
1985-90	10,6	8,5	14,6	8,6	7,1	7,9	9,4
1990-95	11,2	8,0	14,4	8,5	6,5	7,6	9,1
1995-00	11,5	7,6	13,8	8,5	6,1	7,4	8,8

Table 4.3. (Cont'd)

Year	Europe	Asia	Africa	N.America	L.America	Oceania	World
2000-05	11,6	7,1	13,2	8,4	6,0	7,0	8,4
2005-10	11,3	7,0	11,8	8,1	5,9	6,8	8,1

Birth rate, death rate (/1000) 1950-2010

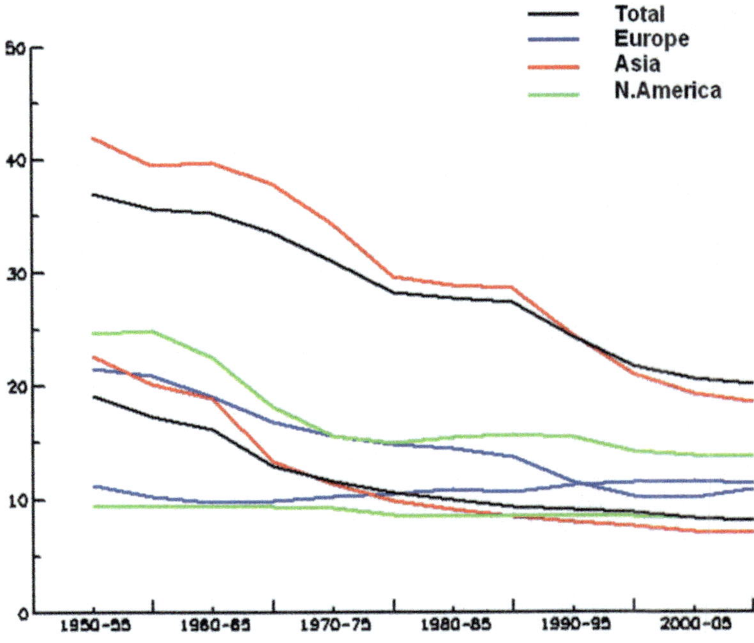

Figure 4.3. UN data for the birth and death rates in the world (black) and in several parts of the world (colors)

It can be seen that the birth rate has decreased significantly all over the world in these 60 years, although Africa is lagging, while the death rate has also decreased, although it seems to be reaching its limits. In fact, in Europe it has been increasing since 50 years ago, due to the ageing of its population. In fact, in Europe the birth rate is now (and has been during the last 15 years) below the death rate. This effect is to be expected rather sooner than later in the other parts of the world, except in Africa, where there is still quite a significant margin, with a growth rate still near 2.5% in 2010, although it reached its peak around 1985 and has come down later. Figure 4.3 shows the birth and death rates for the World, Europe, Asia and North America.

Life expectancy

Table 4.4 and Figure 4.4 show the UN data about life expectancy[5].

Table 4.4. UN data for life expectancy in the world and its main divisions, 1950-2010

Year	Europe	Asia	Africa	N.America	L.America	Oceania	World
1950-55	63,6	42,2	37,4	68,6	51,4	60,4	46,9
1955-60	67,1	44,6	39,9	69,7	54,4	62,4	49,4
1960-65	69,2	46,3	42,3	70,2	56,9	63,9	51,1
1965-70	70,0	54,4	44,4	70,5	58,9	65,0	56,5
1970-75	70,6	57,7	46,5	71,4	61,0	66,4	58,8
1975-80	71,0	60,1	48,7	73,3	63,2	68,2	60,7
1980-85	71,6	62,1	50,6	74,5	65,2	70,2	62,4

Table 4.4. (Cont'd)

Year	Europe	Asia	Africa	N.America	L.America	Oceania	World
1985-90	72,8	64,0	51,8	75,0	67,2	70,9	64,0
1990-95	72,6	65,4	51,7	75,8	68,9	72,5	64,8
1995-00	73,1	66,7	52,1	76,6	70,7	73,7	65,6
2000-05	73,8	68,8	52,9	77,4	72,1	75,3	67,1
2005-10	75,3	70,3	55,6	78,4	73,4	76,8	68,7

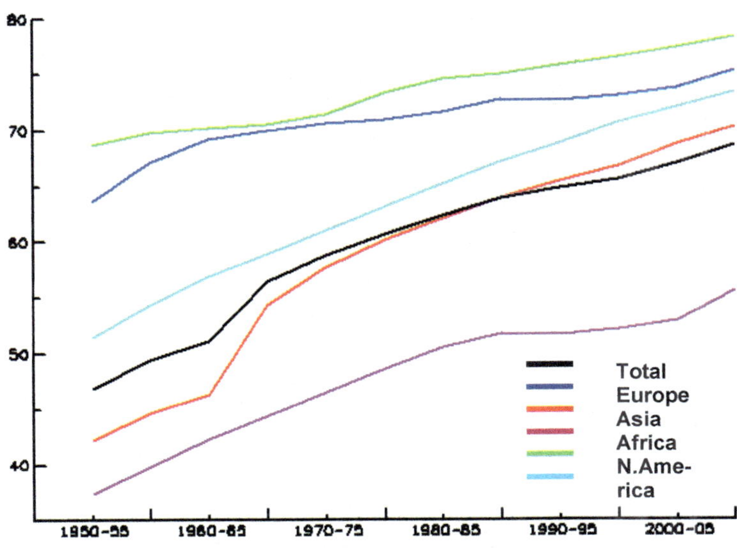

Figure 4.4. UN data for life expectancy in the world (black) and in parts of the world (colors)

It can be seen that life expectancy is increasing in the whole world and every part of it, although in Europe and Africa it seems to have stopped growing in some extent between 1985 and 2005. In the case of Africa the reason could be the enormous spread of AIDS. The European case is more difficult to interpret.

REFERENCES

[1] United Nations, The world at six billion, http://www.un.org/esa/population/publications/sixbillion/sixbilpart1.pdf.
[2] United Nations, Department of Economic and Social Affairs, World Population Prospects: The 2012 Revision.
http://esa.un.org/unpd/wpp/Excel-Data/population.htm.
[3] Gonzalo, J.A., Muñoz, F.F., Santos, D.J., 2012. Using a rate equation approach to model world population trends. Simulation 89(2), 192-198, DOI:10.1177/0037549712463736.
[4] United Nations, Department of Economic and Social Affairs, World Population Prospects: The 2012 Revision.
http://esa.un.org/unpd/wpp/Excel-Data/fertility.htm.
[5] United Nations, Department of Economic and Social Affairs, World Population Prospects: The 2012 Revision.
http://esa.un.org/unpd/wpp/Excel-Data/mortality.htm.

CHAPTER 5
WORLD ECONOMIC EXPANSION: 1945-1990

by Julio A. Gonzalo

Antecedents and subsequent developments

In spite of many international conflicts and two World Wars in the period preceding 1945, world population was increasing at a moderate rate. At the same time, world economy, still partially localized, witnessed continuous ups and downs culminating in the Great Depression of 1929. That Great Depression affected, mainly, Europe, North America and, of course, secondarily, the rest of the world.

The conflict between liberal capitalism and revolutionary socialism, which initially adopted various competing forms (Russian Communism, Italian Fascism, German National Socialism) triggered World War II and displaced the former dominant European powers (England, France, Germany...) from hegemony. After 1945, world hegemony was disputed between the *US* (basically a Christian country with a large Catholic minority) with a group of allied European countries, and the *Soviet Union*, with a group of neighboring (forcefully occupied) countries, and after 1948 with China. The Vatican, which had no military force but had still a considerable moral authority with many millions of Catholics all over Europe, opposed Soviet Communism, which was bloodily persecuting Christians (Catholic or not) at the other side of the "iron curtain."

World economic order (or disorder) is determined by competing national entities (states) within free markets, with capital forces and work forces (in *low*-wage areas and high-wage areas), as well as by political forces trying to control the work force, often against religious and traditional cultural forces. For a very long time, modern states have been getting stronger and stronger, with political forces increasingly more capable of controlling cultural forces, nationalism vs. socialism, traditional religion vs. "scientism," localism vs. universalism, which are in general used rather than served by the political establishment. After the French Revolution, and even before, after the Protestant Reformation, the Christian background which nourished[1] the universities and the institutions of Europe and the Americas was clearly on the defensive… At the same time, the scientific revolution of the 18th and 19th centuries culminated in the first third of the 20th and blossomed immediately in an unprecedented technological revolution which was accompanied by a tremendous increase in agricultural and industrial capacity, and almost a quadrupling of world population between the 1940's and the second decade of the 21th century. As pointed out in Chap. 7, widespread generalization of contraception and abortion in Europe and North America from the 1960's, aggressively pushed throughout the world by Planned Parenthood and the UN for decades, resulted in a drastic decrease of population growth which inevitably will entail a decrease in population and in economy activity by the second half or the 21th century.

In the last two decades, according to Encyclopaedia Britannica[2], the World Gross Income has increased by 63.3% from a WGI of 21.2×10^{12} (*Book of the Year 1992*) to a WGI of 57.8×10^{12} (*Book of the Year 2011*). In the same period, world population increased 20.7%, from 5.4×10^9 (*Book of the Year 1992*) to 6.8×10^9 (*Book of the Year 2011*). In the next two decades *population* will increase much more slowly (just before beginning to decrease) and *gross income* will probably also begin to decrease.

The 1945-1967/73 period

After World War II the US became the world number one military power, the first nuclear power, and thereafter the main nuclear power, up to the end of the "cold war." The protracted conflict of the US with the Soviet Union lasted for more than four decades.

After the Second World War[3], all of the other major industrial economies had been very seriously damaged. As a consequence of the "cold war," large colonial areas in Africa and Asia, including some important oil and gas producing countries, became unstable, with Russia and America competing to displace the former European colonial powers. In fact, the decolonization process, formally supervised by the UN, was disorderly and often chaotic, and some African territories were soon in worst economic conditions than before decolonization. Local wars and conflicts multiplied.

In the 1945-1953 period, the Soviet Union occupied *de facto* large territories in Eastern and Central Europe, at first with the tacit agreement of the US, England and France (remember Yalta and Potsdam). Early in those years the Communist parties of France and Italy were very strong. Spain, after a decisive civil war, which was the prelude to the World War, was strongly anticommunist. And the US, after getting heavily involved in the war of Korea, organized NATO as an anti-Communist defensive alliance. NATO was complemented significantly with the US-Spain military agreements, with important and strategically located air and naval bases, which played a decisive role all along the "cold war" process.

The US set the rules of world economic trade in those post-war years through the Open Door Trading policy, specifically ordained to foster the unity of non-Communist world markets, based upon multilateralism and supressing barriers to the transfer of goods and capital across national borders. The US sought, therefore, the establishment of multilateral economic integration and cooperation under US leadership.

The *Marshall Plan* was instrumental in bringing about the (West) *German* reconstruction and "economic" miracle and the *Italian* recovery and parallel economic "miracle." Ten years later, as the Marshall Plan did not benefit Spain directly, a *Spanish* economic "miracle," in a more modest scale, took place.

The reconstruction of post-war West Germany and post-war Japan led to a revival of industrial activity and to the expansion of the capitalist world economy.

The *Breton Woods* agreements helped to balance payment problems between the US, Europe and Asia.

US military expenditures during the Korean war (the first post-war act of containment) increased by 300%. As a consequence, the prices of primary commodities increased by 150%, allowing Europe and Japan to earn dollars from their trade with the peripheral countries.

The US aid to the French in Indochina in the mid fifties was intended to contain the Russian and Chinese ambitions in the Pacific Rim. This led directly to the protracted Vietnam War, another war of containment against Communist aggression.

The *UN* served as a concrete institutionalization of the idea of world government on a multinational basis. In theory, the UN were a promise for the people in the *peripheral countries*, all over Asia, Africa and South America, to enjoy a large measure of independence, progress and equality. Unfortunately it did not work very well. The UN played a relatively constructive role in quenching out local military conflicts. But its moral authority, which at the beginning had a healthy inspiration in natural law and classical Christian values and was expressed in the declaration of human rights, child's rights, etc., in later years became increasingly anti-family and pro-abortion.

In 1955, the Bandung Conference, inspired by Yugoslavia and other purportedly neutral countries, gave birth to a global non-aligned movement.

During the "cold war" the US promoted (with various degrees of success) economic development as an alternative to Communism. In the late 1960's the US had a $10 billion dollar trade surplus[4] of exports over imports. A few years later, the situation had reversed completely; the US had a $10 billion trade gap of imports over exports. The printing of dollars by the US to pay for the war in Vietnam led to inflation, which led to other countries to cash their dollars against US gold, provoking a crisis which forced the US off the *gold standard* in 1971.

The 1967/73-1990 period

After the Tet Offensive in the Vietnam War, the US hegemony declined in relative terms and the global economy contracted. The *Nixon Doctrine* ended the period in which the US had been in the first line of containment against international Communism, right after the Korean War. That doctrine put occasionally in the front line against Communism other countries, such as Brazil, Israel and South Africa. The early 1970's witnessed the growing power of large scale oil producing countries, which began to accumulate large quantities of *petro-dollars*. The boom in dollars was sent by the US via Western banks to industrializing countries throughout the world.

After the US opened with China an important strategic initiative which definitely broke Chinese-Russian economic and military relationships, there was a heavy chemical and industrial development programmes in the so called far East "little dragons" (South Korea, Hong Kong, Taiwan). After 1970, Third World states increased considerably their military spending, from $4 billion per year in the

1960's to \$40 million in the 1980's. On the other hand, UN peacekeeping missions increased steadily from 1956 up through the present.

Social unrest increased throughout the world in the 1970's, culminating in the 1979 Iranian revolution, which the Carter administration handled very ineptly. During the 1980's the Soviet Union invaded Afghanistan and became involved in a costly war, difficult to win, with heavy indirect US involvement in support of the rebels. The Afghan War, the Chernobyl nuclear disaster, Polish Solidarnosk movement (supported by Pope John Paul II and US president Ronald Reagan) compounded with systemic and insurmountable economic problems, determined the fall of the Soviet Empire.

During the 1980's the US increased expenditure to over \$3 trillion dollars in order to confront the USSR and contain Soviet inspired revolutionary activity in the so called Third World. The unprecedented military build up resulted in a US deficit, but was eminently successful in defeating Soviet Communism.

During the 1980's the US economy[5] grew more slowly than the economies of its major trading partners. Between 1981 and 1988 the US sold \$342 billion dollars worth of arms, 69% going to the Middle East. George Bush (father) found it necessary to revive multilateral alliance to form the first Gulf War coalition.

With one of the Super Powers out of combat, new threats to world order emerged: terrorist groups, specially "fundamentalist" Islamic terrorism carried out unanticipated acts of mass destruction.

The US spent \$1.25 trillion dollars between 1995 and 2000 to build up the military means to confront these new threats and soon reached a deficit above \$4 trillion.

Global possibilities: 1990-2025

The world either will continue evolving more or less as it has evolved for the last century, with constant adjustments, or it will enter a long period of chaos. A crash of prices bringing down inefficient and unprofitable business and corporations is a distinct possibility. An acute increase in social unrest fuelled up by various forms of terrorism, crime, wild protests and intermittent conflicts is not unlikely. From the economic point of view, world economy appears to have now four dynamic poles: North America (US and Canada); the so called "little dragons" (Japan, South Korea and South-East Asia); the European Union; and China.

Nuclear weapons are not out of reach for some developing countries. And the Arab-Israeli conflict continues.

If world economies contract in the first quarter of the 21th century, there will be government cutbacks in social services. For the first time in two centuries the cutbacks will affect the middle classes in the core countries and in the periphery. Diminished expectations will be a major blow to social unity and international peaceful coexistence. Very likely, increased police order will be necessary in the core countries. Unmet expectations of the middle and lower classes will likely result in social tensions.

In an "atheist" perspective, both individual men and world civilizations are seen as the subject of "chance" and "necessity." Population growth and population extinction are meaningless, as everything else under the Sun. In a biblical perspective, however, men have been created by God for a purpose. They have been endowed by the Creator with intelligence, will and freedom, which they can use rightly or wrongly. They are bound in conscience, explicitly or implicitly, by the Ten Commandments.

Alexis Carrel[6], a distinguished Nobel Prize winner and a convert to Catholicism, pointed out in *Man, the Unknown* that, in denying the supremacy of spiritual values, our civilization is making a regression to barbaric times. Only if our civilization recovers respect for human life and human spiritual values it will be able to overcome the unhealthy demographic trend in which we find it at present.

REFERENCES

[1] S. L. Jaki, *Scientist and Catholic: Pierre Duhem* (Beauchesne Editeur: Paris, 1990).

[2] *Encyclopaedia Britannica*: Books of the Year 1992-2011.

[3] See f.i. Immanuel Wallenstein, *The Age of Transition: Trajectory of the World System, 1945-2025*: Terence R. Hopkins, Immanuel Maurice Wallenstein Books.

[4] *Ibidem*: 1945-1967/73.

[5] *Ibidem*: 1967/73-1990.

[6] Alexis Carrel, *Man, the Unknown* (New York and London: Harper and Brothers, 1935); *The Voyage to Lourdes* (New York: Harper and Row, 1939).

CHAPTER 6
ENERGY, POPULATION AND THE ENVIRONMENT
by Julio A. Gonzalo

Table 6.1 shows 2004 data for the population, *total energy consumption* (Mtoe), *per capita energy consumption* (Kgtoe) and *per capita* gross national product (US$) for the twenty main consumer countries in the world[1,2], ordered by Mtoe.

Table 6.1. Total and per capita energy consumption
(For the world twenty main consumer countries)

Country	Population	Total E.C.	Per Capita E.C.	GNP
	(Millions)	(Mtoe)	(Kgtoe)	US $
USA	293	2325	7935	37610
China	1529	1609	1052	1100
Russia	144	642	4458	2610
India	1081	573	530	530
Japan	127	533	4196	34510
Germany	82	348	4243	25250
France	60	275	4583	24770
Canada	31	266	8540	23930
UK	59	234	3966	28350
South Korea	48	213	4437	12020

Table 6.1. (Cont'd)

Country	Population	Total E.C.	Per Capita E.C.	GNP
	(Millions)	(Mtoe)	(Kgtoe)	US $
Brazil	180	205	1138	2710
Italy	57	184	3228	21560
Indonesia	222	174	783	600
Mexico	105	165	1571	6230
Iran	67	146	2179	2000
Spain	43	142	3302	16990
Saudi Arabia	24	140	5712	6900
Ukraine	47	140	2978	970
South Africa	46	131	2817	3170
Australia	20	116	5800	21650

China's total energy consumption, which thirty years before was a relatively small fraction (a few percent) of the world total, became comparable to the US Mtoe in 2004, and is increasing yearly. *India*'s Mtoe, completely negligible thirty years before, became almost one fourth of the US Mtoe in 2004, and keeps increasing. So, important changes are to be expected for the future.

In 2005, the energy *consumed* by OECD countries was mainly obtained from coal, oil and gas (83%), from nuclear and hydroelectric centrals (13%) and from renewable sources (just 4%).

Worldwide renewable sources produced in 2005 only 184 Gwatt, distributed as follows:

36% small scale hydroelectric
32% wind
24% biomass
 5% geothermal
 3% solar

In particular, the five countries with greatest *wind energy* installed capacity (Gwatt) were Germany 18.4, Spain 10.0, USA 9.2, India 4.4, and Denmark 3.1. Not too much, certainly.

For the time being (2011), most of these *renewable* energy sources are expensive and inconvenient. And there are problems also coming from the more *conventional* energy sources: scarcity of oil and gas in the near future; growing concern about "global warming" (with or without a serious justification), due to CO_2 emissions from coal, oil and gas; unexpected accidents (earthquakes, tsunamis) in nuclear plants, like those that took place in Japan (Fukushima Daiichi plant), the Gulf of Mexico oil spill, etc. In times of crisis, however, it is good to remember that in the past, crisis were not lacking.

The economics of conventional and alternative energy sources

As it is well known[3], oil and natural gas are the world's most widely used energy sources and probably the most valuable. Since the oil price peaks in the 1970's, engineers and scientists have attempted to find alternatives in order to become less oil dependent. Environmental considerations and concerns about global warming, exaggerated by some and downplayed by others, are nowadays playing a definitive role.

Critics[4] of "global warming" say that satellite global measurements in the Southern hemisphere between 1980 and 2000, after smoothing out, indicate a linear increase of 0.058 °C/decade. This is not too much, having into account that, according to UN-IPCC-2001, historical estimates for the last millennium indicate long term oscillations in the average Earth's temperature of $\pm$ 1°C, with a warm medieval period roughly from 1100 to 1400, followed by a little "ice age" from 1500 to 2000, apparently followed by another relatively warm period beginning at the present. So, these critics say "global warming" is not man made, not catastrophic, and not global. On the other hand, the opposite side insists[5] that the world's car population has grown five times as fast as the human population over the last 50 years, with serious environmental consequences, including "global warming."

Most oil alternatives have not been up to now very successful, probably due, among other things, to what are called "economies of scale." Most of those oil alternatives have poor physical characteristics, creating a loss in economies of scale. Consequently, during the world transition from oil to oil alternatives, economic growth may go down, and the world economy may suffer a serious decline. Technology, in order to be successful, must overcome its own obviously disadvantageous physical characteristics. Oil alternatives should develop an extremely large increase in their productivity. In the long run, a "hydrogen" based economy, using a variety of conventional and alternative resources and hydrogen as the energy carrier ($H_2O + energy \Leftrightarrow H_2 + O_2$) may be the best solution. Energy release and energy storage in a "hydrogen economy" would take place with efficiencies of the order of 85%. This is very attractive, even if fusion energy research is finally successful in producing lots of clean and cheap energy.

Nuclear energy safety after the Fukushima disaster

The hundreds of nuclear reactors operating around the world are under scrutiny after the nuclear disaster in Japan's four crippled reactors[6] at the Fukushima Daiichi plant due to the 11 march earthquake and tsunami.

The US, China and France have a considerable stake in the future of nuclear power. As Japanese workers worked strenuously to bring under control the crippled reactors, other nations launched safety assessment of their nuclear plants –while reassuring the population that a repeat of the sequence of events that led to the accidents in the Japanese reactors was highly unlikely, the closure of operating facilities and the eventual abandonment of nuclear energy, with a few exceptions, was not seriously considered.

The US

The US is the home of the largest number of commercial reactors in the world. The Nuclear Regulatory Commission (NRC) assembled a task force of senior managers and former staff experts within days of the March 11 earthquake. Within three months, the task force would recommend possible formal changes to the NRC regulation.

The NRC executive director for operations told a recent Senate hearing that the Commission has recently approved a 20-year license extension for more than half of the 104 operating US reactors. The Vermont Yankee plant, one of the 23 US units with the same General Electric Mark I boiling-water reactor (BWR) design as the four crippled reactors at the Fukushima Daiichi plant, with their spent-fuel pools, was granted an extension just days after the accident. The Vermont reactor was initially licensed for 40 years in 1972.

According to Bill Borchardt, NREC executive director, there is no reason to slow down the relicensing process. If a change to the design of a US plant is called for by what has been learned from the Fukushima accident, the NCR would order that change to be made outside the licensing process. Additional safety requirements should likely be addressed to prevent a prolonged loss-of-coolant crisis like the one which took place at the Fukushima reactors. In the aftermath of the 9/11 terrorist attack on New York Twin Towers, the NCR undertook a review of the spent-fuel pool vulnerability issue specific to BWR. As a result, measures to ensure that adequate water levels are maintained in the pools were greatly enhanced.

Other NCR requirements are intended to mitigate the likelihood of the power blackouts and the hydrogen build-ups that caused the explosions and radiation leaks in the Japan BWR. The requirements include the installation of radiation-hardened vent systems to release containment pressure and the better positioning of batteries and other key pieces of equipment that would have helped operators at Fukushima to regain control of the reactors more safely within hours after the earthquake.

Only one of the 62 reactors now under construction in the world is in the US. In 20101 its completion was scheduled for 2013. In the US, another 9 reactors are presently planned and 23 are proposed. Present plans supporting more nuclear power, as part of an effort to increase the US electricity generated from "clean energy" sources, do not seem to be under question for the moment, but the building of new reactors will depend on the level of public acceptance and on the availability of financing. High costs, frequent overruns and regulatory uncertainties are large, however, for nuclear plants, compared with plants using natural gas and coal.

China

China's Premier Wen Jiabao suspended the review process for new reactor projects in China a few days after the Fukushima disaster. Safety reviews were ordered for the 13 operating plants now existing in China, to assess contingencies such as floods, earthquakes and other natural disasters. Chinese authorities insisted that the country's nuclear expansion plans would remain on track. Yu Zusheng, a qualified official of the Ministry of Environmental Protection, was reported to say to *China Economic Weekly* that China would increase the use of third generation reactor designs, such as a Westinghouse's AP 1000, which include passively safe systems that require no water pumps to cool the core in an emergency shutdown. 28 of the 61 reactors under construction worldwide are located in China and another 50 reactors are planned to begin construction within 10 years. Additional 110 reactors are being considered for China within about 15 years, according to the World Nuclear Association (WNA).

Europe

In Europe, political leaders reached a consensus on the need for international nuclear safety standards in the wake of Japan's power plant disaster. French President Nicolas Sarkozy visited Tokyo in March 31st 2011 and said he was inviting in May the group of the 20 more developed nations to Paris, to discuss the matter of nuclear safety. France's investments in nuclear energy have been great since the end of World War Two. 75% of the country's electricity needs, more than any other nation in the world, is produced in France's 58 reactors. And France was selling more than 3 billion euros ($ 4.3 billion) worth of power annually to its neighbours.

European Union ministers met on May 21st and announced plans to carry out tests to evaluate the safety of the 143 reactor now operating in EU member states. Voluntary tests should get under way by the end of the year in the member states, to assess seismic and flooding vulnerabilities, in particular, the adequacy of reactor cooling, backup electricity supply systems and other factors. British Prime Minister David Cameron said the tests should be performed by independent international regulators, and German Chancellor Angela Merkel called for the results to be made public. The disparity of views, however, between the 27 EU member states (14 of which use now commercial nuclear power plants) is considerable. Italy, for instance, which had closed the last of its four commercial power plants in 1990, had plans underway to build four new reactors in 2013. The German government, on the other hand, was considering whether to close its 17 reactors and abandon nuclear power altogether. Within days of the quake in Japan, German authorities ordered the shutdown of the 7 oldest commercial reactors in the country, all of them commissioned before 1980. The 19 British commercial reactors in operation were put under a six month safety review. In the UK, nuclear energy accounts for 18% of the electricity output according to the WNA. Labour government in the UK had set in 2006 a new national policy aimed at nuclear growth.

On March 28th, the International Atomic Energy Agency general director, Yukiya Amano, announced the convening of a nuclear safety conference in Vienna for June 20-24th, with an agenda devoted to assess the causes and consequences of the Fukushima disaster, strengthening nuclear safety and recommending accident response measures.

The 2011 report of the Gulf Oil Spill Commission

Cherry Murray[7], Dean of the Harvard School of Engineering and Applied Sciences, and President of the American Physical Society in 2009, served on the National Commission on the British Petroleum (BP) Deepwater Horizon Oil Spill and Offshore Drilling, established in May 2010 by President Obama, to study the Gulf of Mexico Oil Spill and its consequences. The main objective of the

Commission was to take a look at the whole picture and then to develop options for guarding against and mitigating oil spills associated with offshore drilling, as well as to learn from the Gulf of Mexico disasters and to figure out what government, industry and whoever else might be involved, in order to prevent such large scale disasters to happen again in the future. The Commission asked the industry for improvements in human safety as well as a strengthening in the oil spill response, by planning in advance the containment of oil wells. Then the Commission looked at what to do about restoring the Gulf, and to the financial responsibilities of the parties at fault.

The major conclusion was that the incident was a failure of industry management and a government oversight. Offshore oil drilling can be done safely. It will always have risks, but according to Murray, it is possible to mitigate those risks. She was in three subcommittees, those which dealt with what actually happened at the well; industry safety; and containment, the three most engineering oriented committees. Since five US states were involved in the disaster, the committee members fanned out to look at the impact on the local governments, on the people and on other entities in the Gulf. They did a quick tour and held a hearing in New Orleans for several days. The investigative lawyer team went down with the sister ship, the Deepwater Nautilus, leased by Shell and owned by Transocean, to look at what it would be like being on the rig, and to see exactly what is where, because the Commission was trying to figure out *who knew what when.* The Commission was bipartisan: one of the two co-chairs a Republican, the other one a Democrat. Obviously, many lawsuits are going to start from this accident. In the middle of an incredible political and legal situation, the Commission had to do its work as best as possible. It was clear to the Commission that the past oversight demanded a complete revamping of the procedures.

As noted by Cherry Murray, the Gulf region in the five states affected by the Oil Spill has a predominantly family-centered culture. Each family is involved in one of three things: tourism, fishing, and oil exploitation (providing services, or working on the oil rigs). The Coast Guard was doing a fantastic job according to Murray, but there was a communication problem. The locals, who felt completely left out, were added later *ad hoc* to the teams. "The nation learned the lesson that we need better local involvement in the response to the incident," said Professor Murray. "The technology that the oil and gas industry uses to drill these wells in very deep water is comparable in sophistication to the technology to go into space. What they have not done is put as many energy and resources in the safety and containment technology and the response to the spill, and that has to change." The only way to kill for good an oil well takes now 90 days. Something better is needed. Self-policing and much better oversight are needed.

World population and energy consumption limits

Is there an *upper limit* to world *population* in our planet?

The availability of *food* and *water* is heavily dependent on the availability of *energy*. It might be conjectured that in the relatively distant future, with a population *thirty* or *forty times* the present world population, our planet could be approaching that *limit*. If such were the case, common sense, supported by elementary rational and healthy religious considerations, could recommend the *natural fertility regulation* of births, which is perfectly compatible with an average distribution of the number of children per family, resulting in an *average* number of children per woman in the interval 2.1 – 2.4, depending on the circumstances. For instance, if 10% women have no children, 10% one child, 40% two, 20% three, 10% four, and less than 5% five or more, the resulting average would be 2.25 children per woman, i.e. *replacement level*, about the same as the world average in the year 2000.

As the effects of the growing sexual promiscuity brought up by the generalized use of contraceptives (the pill, condoms, DIUs, etc.) are becoming more notorious, *natural methods* of fertility regulation are beginning to be more appreciated. Not yet, however, as much as they deserve. At the International Conference on Population and Development held at *El Cairo* in 1994, Dr. Kevin Hume and Dr. Rosario Cabañas, of *WOOMB International*, made a compact and effective presentation of the many advantages of the Billings[8] Method of *Natural Family Planning* (NFP).

WOOMB had, at the time, branches in 44 countries. The method is taught woman-to-woman in all these countries. It was estimated in 1987 that about 50 million couples were using the method worldwide, on both sides of the Iron Curtain. There are no catholic ovaries and communist ovaries; nor white, black or yellow ovaries. In Australia, where Drs. Billings, wife and husband, were born, the Government has recognized their valuable contribution to public health. About 70% Australian couples have been trained in the Billings NFP method, which is frequently used as a possible solution to infertility problems.

The method's philosophy aims to responsible maternity and paternity, promoting effectively stable and happy families. Economic cost is negligible and no specialized professional training is required for its implementation. Women in undeveloped countries, where primary medical assistance is almost non-existent, can benefit greatly from knowing their own natural fertility cycles as provided by the Billings ovulation method.

More than 50 million women in more than 100 countries are benefitting from the advantages that the Billings method provides.

From the point of view of human dignity there is little question that NFP helps to put human sexuality in its proper place, instead of reducing it to a purely genital relationship.

REFERENCES

[1] Dan Smith, *The Penguin State of the World Atlas*, 8th edition (Penguin Books: London, 2008).

[2] See f.i. Encyclopaedia Britannica, Books of the Year 1990-2010.

[3] D. B. Reynolds, Scarcity and Growth Considering Oil and Energy (The Edwin Mellen Press: Lewiston, New York, 2002).

[4] Chris C. Horner, The Politically Incorrect Guide to Global Warming (Regnery Publishing, Inc.: Washington, 2007).

[5] Dan Smith, ibidem, p. 114.

[6] David Kramer, Physics Today (May 2011).

[7] APS News (8 May, 2001), "The Back Page: The Gulf Oil Spill Commission: An Inside Look," Cherry Murray interviewed by Michael Lucibella.

[8] See, f.i., O. Velez, L. Guerra and J. A. Gonzalo, El futuro de la población mundial (Ciencia y Cultura: Madrid, 2008).

SECTION 2

IS THE EARTH OVERPOPULATED?

CHAPTER 7
ABORTION AND POPULATION CONTROL[*]
by Julio A. Gonzalo and Colin Clark

Colin Clark (1905-1989) was a British-Australian world renowned economist. Born in London and educated in Oxford and Winchester, he graduated in Chemistry in 1928. He worked in the following entities:

- London School of Economics (1928-29).
- University of Liverpool (1929-30).
- Research assistant to the Economic Advisory Council (1930).
- Lecturer at Cambridge University (1930-38).
- Government Statistician, Director of the Bureau of Industry, and Financial Advisor to Queensland Treasury (1938-42).
- Deputy Director of the Commonwealth Department of War Organisation of Industry (Queensland, 1942-46).
- Under Secretary of the Queensland Department of Labour and Industry (1947-51).
- Member of the Food and Agriculture Organization in Rome (1951).
- Director of the Institute for Agricultural Economics at Oxford University (1952–69).
- Director of the Institute of Economic Progress at Monash University (1969–78).

---

[*] Colin Clark, *Abortion and Population*, Human Life Review, Summer, 1976.

• Research Consultant to the Department of Economics at the University of Queensland (1978- 89).

His important book "Conditions of Economic Progress" was published in 1940.

In 1984 he was chosen by the World Bank as one of the "pioneers of development."

His article on "Abortion and Population" in Human Life Review (summer, 1976) is reprinted with permission below:

***

It is not my custom to comment on articles in the *American Journal of Obstetrics and Gynecology* (though this journal is welcome to comment on any article of mine). But this convention may perhaps be waived when a leading article does not deal with obstetrics and gynecology, but with politics and economics.

The article in question (October 15, 1975) was the presidential address to the American Gynecological Society by Dr. Louis M. Hellman, M.D., who holds official rank in the Federal Department of Health, Education and Welfare as Deputy Assistant Secretary.

What is novel about Dr. Hellman's address is that, after the usual fervent demands for population limitation, he goes on not only to tolerate, but actively to demand abortion. "No country has reduced its population growth significantly without resorting to abortion… Despite the Supreme Court decision in 1973 legalizing abortions… the issue remains morally and ethically controversial. Public debate continues with an increasing number of legal actions and a variety of proposed legislation. Neither family planning nor AID funds can be used to support or promote abortion."

Dr. Hellman also mentions sterilization, sometimes enforced by legal, or pseudo-legal, means. "We physicians," he admits, "have been incredibly lax in the matter, and in rare instances outright cavalier."

"When I joined the Federal Government five years ago," states Dr. Hellman, "population and family planning were subjects of high priority to both the administration and the Congress. In the last few years, however, I sense a diminishing concern among our own people and our own Government about our own population problem, which many believe to be solved, and the world issues ... the national will to face population issues continues to falter." "Retrenchment of federally funded support... for family planning" will, we are told, "threaten national security."

It may be added that the Government of India, after receiving world-wide publicity for its program of mass sterilization of men in return for a small sum of money or a transistor radio, found that this program had only a limited effect and was unpopular—politicians addressing meetings were faced by hecklers who asked if they themselves had been sterilized. Recently India also has reduced expenditure on its family limitation program.

The phrase "zero population growth" can have two very different meanings. One is actual equality of births and deaths, i.e., zero population growth in the literal sense. The alternative meaning is that the average family should be at replacement level (i.e., just sufficient to replace the parental generation).

What constitutes replacement level varies of course with circumstances. The principal factor to be taken into account is the proportion of children who may be expected to die before themselves reaching maturity. Thus, among primitive tribesmen, average completed families of six may only just constitute replacement level. In modern communities however an allowance of only three or four percent need be made for children dying before reaching maturity. Then an allowance must be made for the minority of women who will remain unmarried—that is, if we are considering the required average offspring per marriage. Finally—a factor often forgotten—we must allow for the male surplus at birth. On an average (for biological reasons not known) there are 1.06 male births for every one female. So, even if there were no child mortality, and no women remained unmarried, it would still require 2.06 offspring to replace two parents. Taking all factors into account, it appears that an average of about 2.2 offspring per marriage is required to replace the parental generation. The U.S.A. appears now to be at or perhaps below this level. (The determination, from currently available statistics, of expected average final completed family is an awkward problem in mathematics, for the solution of which several alternative methods are available. Solution is not helped by the extremely late publication of some important vital statistics).

Some people still find it difficult to grasp the proposition that, if births are actually equal to deaths, population in the future is certain to decline, for the simple reason that births will then only be replacing the much smaller generation born on the average some sixty or seventy years ago. (The only exception to this rule would be a country like Ireland, where the generation born sixty or seventy years ago was *larger* than the present generation, so current equality between births and deaths would mean that the population would be certain to increase—if they did not emigrate).

So we have the concept of "demographic momentum." Dr. Hellman complains that, even with American families now at or below replacement level, some population growth, though gradual, may be expected to continue for the next sixty or seventy years.

For other countries, however, strikingly different results are obtained. General Draper, President Nixon's appointment as U.S.

spokesman on the United Nations' Population Commission, at an international banquet (was this really an appropriate occasion?), made the somewhat undiplomatic statement that not only was the United States adopting the policy of zero population growth but that Latin America was also expected to adopt the same policy by the end of the century. But he did not specify which of the two meanings of the phrase zero population growth he had in mind. M. Bourgeois-Pichat, Director of the French Demographic Institute, made calculations on the two different meanings. If the intention was that Latin American births should literally equal deaths by the end of the century, the average Latin American family, which is now about six, would immediately have to be reduced to about one-tenth of its present size. If, on the more plausible but still extremely unlikely assumption that it was expected that the average Latin American family should fall to replacement size by the end of the century, the demographic momentum of the young people already growing up would still cause Latin American population to go on increasing until well past the middle of next century, eventually stabilizing at about three times its present level.

One of the principal reasons for the "faltering" of which Dr. Hellman complains in the United States is the strong opposition now expressed by spokesmen for blacks and other minorities. This has generated an acute crisis in the minds of many fashionable Leftists, who regard themselves as pro-black, but who think that the best service that they can render to blacks is to reduce their numbers.

The "population community"[1](rather an odd title for those whose whole concern is to reduce population) at its First National Congress on Optimum Population and Environment, "was taught a hard lesson by... the blacks who attended the sessions... not firebrand militants but representatives of relatively conservative groups such as Planned Parenthood and the National Urban League... on the last day of the congress the entire black caucus walked out." Some black spokesmen complain that officially sponsored family limitations represents a deliberate attempt to check their increasing relative numbers, indeed of "genocide."

In the 1880's the pioneer French sociologist Arsène Dumont made the important observation that racial, linguistic, or religious minorities always tended to be more reproductive than the majorities which surrounded them. The reason for this was, simply, that seeing little prospect of social or economic advancement for their children, they had less incentive to limit their number. Dumont observed this among the Basque, Breton, and Italian-speaking minorities in his own country. It is true alike of the American blacks, of Australian aborigines, of Chinese settlers throughout South-East Asia, and of Indian migrants to Guyana, East Africa, and Fiji—in the last-named case, to the point where the minority eventually became the majority.

The outstanding exception, of course, the "exception which tests the rule," is the case of the Jews, who do not appear to be more reproductive than the Gentile majority which surrounds them. The Jews however are proverbially successful in securing social and economic advancement for their children.

In the international sphere, increasing American indifference, Dr. Hellman complains, "will pose a threat to our leadership role." Well may he complain. Accusations of genocide, etc., have become more strident—as many Americans observed with dismay at the International Population Conference at Bucharest in 1974.

At previous World Population Conferences, the Russian delegates —having conspicuously gone out into the lobby to receive their instructions before they spoke—took a uniform line, namely that Malthusianism was the last, most vicious, and most degraded form of imperialism, designed to destroy the vitality of the peoples of the developing countries. Now our policy in Russia, they continued, is complete economic and social equality for women (including the right, as travelers have observed, to work as builders, labourers, and generally to do most of the heavy work). This having been done, the Russian spokesmen continued, family size fell of its own accord. So far as can be ascertained, the average family in Soviet Russia has now been at or below replacement level for some time and Soviet leaders are clearly concerned. There are, moreover, important regional differences. The Russians, with their keen sense of racial superiority (on which the Chinese have commented unfavorably) observe with dismay the strangely-named non-Russian-speaking peoples of Soviet Asia (Kazakhs, Uzbeks, etc.) continuing to multiply rapidly, while the Soviet Europeans are not replacing themselves.

By the time of the Bucharest Conference the Russian attitude had become more ambiguous, and it was left to the Chinese (in spite of the fact that they are apparently making considerable efforts to reduce their own births, at any rate among the urban population) to take the lead in mobilizing the Third World against the American proposals, which they did with considerable skill. The Conference ended, as will be remembered, with a remarkable alliance between China and the Vatican to oppose these proposals.

The grounds given for the so fervent demands for American and world-wide population limitation are the familiar ones of the supposed inability of the earth to provide food, minerals, and energy for increasing numbers. Attention is drawn to hungry countries such as India, Pakistan, and Bangladesh, where there is little or no additional land for cultivation. But there are countries with much denser populations per acre of agriculture land, such as Japan, Taiwan and Egypt, which succeed in obtaining three times as much rice per unit of land as in the Indian sub-continent. In other Asian countries such as Indonesia, and in almost the whole of Africa and Latin America, there are enormous areas of good potential agricultural land still untouched.

The controversy about the world's capacity to supply food, in which I have been engaged for many years, has now (somewhat to my regret) been brought to an end. Dr. Pawley, formerly head of the FAO Policy Committee, addressing the Scandinavian Economists Conference in 1971 (a summary of his address was given in the FAO Journal *Ceres,* July-August 1971), after making some unfriendly references to my writings, went on to admit that it was far too easy for people like me to criticize FAO, because the truth of the matter was that, in the course of the next hundred years, there should be no serious difficulty about raising food production to thirty or even fifty times what it is now. (Similar conclusions have also recently been published by Wageningen Agricultural University in the Netherlands). My own targets are more modest than these.

In 1949 the United Nations held a world conference on resources, at which I was one of the principal speakers. Recently I looked up the tables of world mineral resources then presented to us, and subtracted from them the amounts which we have in fact already mined since 1949. I find that we have already used up the entire world supplies of copper, lead, zinc, and some other minerals. To treat the proved reserves known to mining companies as estimates of final world resources is ludicrous. Mining companies have to earn dividends for their share-holders, or borrow money at high rates of interest, and therefore they must apply high rates of discount to their expenditure on exploration, which is very costly. They cannot afford to explore for minerals which they do not expect to use more than fifteen years or so in the future.

It is possible that world reserves of oil will run out in fifty years or so—though we have so often been told this before—and recent high oil prices have led to remarkable intensification of oil search, and economies and substitution in use. But available coal reserves will last for very much longer and reserves of uranium and thorium for generating nuclear power longer still. If, for any reason, we dislike the idea of being dependent on nuclear power, the energy reaching the earth each year from the sun is far in excess of any conceivable needs, once we develop the technology for harnessing it.

So far from the threat of over-population, the real threat with which a large part of the world will soon be faced is that of depopulation. In countries such as the U.S., there is no indication that the fall in family size, which has already been reduced to the replacement level, may not continue. In some European countries, particularly Germany, Sweden and Switzerland, births are already a long way below replacement level, and the fall may proceed still further. Since the beginning of the 1960's some much more profound force than the discovery of oral contraceptives (which occurred about this time) has been at work in the Western countries, some feeling of loss of purpose in life, what some social psychologists even call "death-wish."

The reduction in births which has already taken place during the last fifteen years, writes the French historian Pierre Chaunu, will suffice to produce, by the 1990's, a historical disaster worse than the depopulation of Europe by the Black Death.

REFERENCES

[1] Population Reference Bureau, *Population Bulletin* December 1970, pp. 18-19

Chapter 8
Government Family Planning Now and In the Future[*]
by Julio A. Gonzalo and Jacqueline Kasun

Jacqueline Kasun (1924-2009) was a leading conservative woman, professor emeritus of economics at the University of Arkata, California. She had a remarkable life which spanned the globe. She was a devout Christian, a strong and courageous pro-life leader and pro-family advocate. After graduating from the University of California at Berkeley, she enlisted in the U.S. Army. Eventually she earned a Master and a Doctorate at Columbia University. She married Lt. Col. Joseph Kasun and they had two daughters and a son. She was co-founder of Humbolt Pro-Life. Her remarkable book on "The War Against Population" (Ignatius Press, 1st. edition 1988, 2nd revised edition 1999) had a great impact in the U.S. and throughout the world in defense of human life, exposing eloquently the false anti-babies propaganda of such organizations as Planned Parenthood, financed to a very large extent by public money and by big money from international foundations and world organizations. She founded the Grandma House to help pregnant girls in crisis. As she says in her book: "The idea that humanity is multiplying at an accelerating rate is one of the false dogmas of our times…"

In what follows we comment briefly on the last chapter of her book, which is devoted to "Government family planning."

---

[*] Jacqueline Kasun, *The war against population*, Revised Ed,, Ignatius Press: San Francisco,1999.

As Jacqueline Kasun points out, the government's encroachment in the reproductive process has gone too far. So far that it would be almost unbelievable fifty years ago, and hardly believable just fifteen years ago.

The final chapter of Jacqueline's book is very well written and packed with information. With the permission of "Ignatius Press", a compact set of selective quotations may give the reader a good idea.

"The justification for the extent of government involvement in reproductive decisions rests on the contention that the severity of overpopulation in an overcrowded earth demands that people, especially poor people, be educated to control their fertility. The teaching speaks metaphorically of the earth as a "space ship," or "lifeboat." We are, the tale continues, spilling over the edges, and an accretion of more people will sink us all" (2nd. ed.: 279).

The population planners are convinced that human beings, especially the poor and the minorities, are incapable of procreating rationally. For them, this justifies that the administrators of the government assume extraordinary powers through "outreach" and "motivation" programs. But very soon they notice that more coercive measures may be necessary.

"As for the economic claims of the population controllers, they (the lifeboat metaphor among them) disintegrate under examination. Resources, far from being limited, are abounding. No more that 1 to 3 percent of the earth's ice-free land area is occupied by human beings, less than one-ninth is used for agricultural purposes. Eight times and perhaps as much as twenty-two times, the world's present population could support itself at the present standard of living, using presently available technology; and this leaves half the earth's land surface open to wildlife and conservation areas." (2nd edition, p. 281).

As Jacqueline notes, pollution and environmental degradation are not necessarily due to the population growth but, rather, to a lack of political will and to political incompetence. Almost a third of the earth's land surface is covered by forests and in some nations they are presently growing faster than they are being cut. We all know that trees have been cut and have grown throughout history on our planet's surface. And many serious scientists consider the panic about the "global warning" menace as transitory as the previous panic about the "coming ice age." It is not that population causes traffic jams, it is rather, that government economic planning does not work properly.

The claim that a hapless humanity, outbreeding out of control, is falling into misery, is far from true. And the lack of "access" to family-planning "services," which the population planners have been decrying for years, is not true either. If it were, it is difficult to understand why anovulant pills have been piling up for years in the warehouses of Bangladesh, for instance.

"The government family planners aspire not only to exert more control over those whom they ostensibly serve- the young and the poor and the minorities- but also over those who are forced to support the programs by taxation. As an example, the largest private operator of subsidized birth-control clinics, Planned Parenthood, receives little more than a fifth of its support from private voluntary contributions, and part of even that comes from government as payroll-deduction drives among public employees and military personnel. Put succinctly, the government antinatalists have reached the point where they can press their indoctrination and their services on targeted groups of citizens while taxing them for the privilege." (2nd edition, p. 282).

"The real demographic problem of the twenty-first century is likely to be the dwindling proportion of young people relative to the old, which will strain social security systems and cause many other problems." (2nd. Edition, p. 284).

As Jacqueline points out, the inspiration of government birth control is and always has been, eugenic. The booklets of Planned Parenthood, the Gruttmacher Institute and the like are profusely illustrated by dusky women surrounded by lots of children living in slums. The rationale of the eugenic movement is scientific racism. Eugenic policies do not solve social problems, they simply eliminate people.

"The government family-planning programs implicitly, but fundamentally and necessarily, assume that the government can, in its wisdom, correct the "mistakes" of private actions, a faulty assumption all the way around. Individual families have always faced real cost restraints on their behavior, including reproduction, unlike government planners, who do not risk their own resources in their projects but shift the costs of their mistakes to others... From urban unemployment to slow growth and environmental degradation, government planners can lay the blame, not on failed plans, but on "overpopulation"." (2nd. Edition, p. 285).

For family planners, birth control is now and will be in the foreseeable future the final solution to poverty. Their main interest is to maximize the scope of their programs. Planners do not make profits by reducing costs to voluntary buyers, but receive income proportional to the costs they incur in the process of producing goods. It is obvious that it is in the best interest of the subsidized birth control industry to provide as many contraceptives, sterilizations and abortions as possible. To expect otherwise would be to expect them to act against their economic interest.

"The real problem of government family planning is not one of families out of control, but of planners out of control." (2nd. Edition, p. 287).

The planners are inspired by a social philosophy that holds that there is no universal standard of goodness, truth and justice.

The leaders of the population-control movement are the self-appointed interpreters of technological change and social change. They are the enlightened few who are entitled to dictate what changes in beliefs are suitable to the new conditions: the "change agents," the enlightened vanguard guiding humanity towards a new future.

In the Age of Socialism it has become clear, contrary to the views of prominent birth controllers, that the government does not support the people. On the contrary, the people necessarily work and pay taxes to support themselves and the government. Official data do not reflect the care that families give their own. And official policy does discourage or destroy much of the care that voluntary charity has been giving historically to the poor and the less privileged. People must pay heavy taxes to support social programs that do not work. It is not surprising that population controllers seek to accomplish their agenda through the United Nations bureaucracy, which is even further removed than national governments from truly democratic processes. The environmental agencies of the United Nations, in their aspiration to planned and controlled "sustainable development," combine the fervor of nature worship with the lack of accountability of an unelected international bureaucracy, as Jacqueline Kasun eloquently shows.

"The movement has gained momentum in the centers of power; it has captured the subsidized and politicized educational and research systems with its rationalizations; it has its own publishing and advertising outlets; and it has prodigious public funding and reciprocal political support." (2nd Edition, p. 290).

As Jacqueline points out, infanticide (once virtually stamped out in Asia) has now returned and is gaining ground in the West, not only for children with Down's syndrome, but also for social and economic reasons; in the West, the case for the "terminally" ill slips easily from alleviation of discomfort to "merciful" killing; "important" people will be treated with exotic treatments, but the poor, the politically "undistinguished," will be classified as "terminal" and will be given expeditious therapy; current trends toward death instruction will accelerate making these new public "services" as common as birth control.

However, the irony is that world is moving towards a leveling population and possibly a population decline after mid Twenty First Century, as implied by the United Nations demographic projections. The international drive to reduce fertility is an effort to bring about something which is already happening anyway. The efforts of the population planners, besides going against human freedom and human dignity, are already producing and will continue producing unwanted and unexpected consequences.

"Only a radical repudiation of the philosophy of social planning could reverse the trend." (2nd edition, p. 294).

This brief summary does not do justice to the full chapter in Jacqueline Kasun's book, which the interested reader is suggested to consult.

CHAPTER 9
THE RHETORIC OF POPULATION CONTROL: DOES THE END JUSTIFY THE MEANS?[*]

by Julio A. Gonzalo and Julian Simon

Julian Simon (1932-98) was a distinguished American Professor of Economics at the University of Illinois. His book "The Ultimate Resource," published by Princeton University Press (1981), includes a chapter on "The Rhetoric of Population Control."

Simon wrote many books and articles on economic subjects. His work contemplates lasting economic benefits from natural resources and continuous population growth despite limited or finite physical resources. He was involved in the famous Simon – Ehrlich wager, with apocalyptic ecologist Paul R. Ehrlich, who bet that the prices for five metals would increase over a decade, while Simon took the opposite stance. Simon won.

In the next paragraphs we will comment briefly on an adapted version of the chapter of Simon's book mentioned above, published in Human Life Review (Fall, 1983).

"It is a truism by now that resources are getting more scarce, and that population growth exacerbates the problem... So well accepted have these ideas become that eminent people in other fields treat them as assumptions in their own work, on a "everyone knows" basis – the way everyone knows that without sunshine the flowers will not grow" (HLR, Fall 1983, p.62).

---

[*] Julian Simon, *The Economy of Population Growth* (Princeton University Press: Princeton, 1977)

Next Simon lists a long list of personalities who have publicly decried population growth: psychologist O. H. Mowrer; Nobel agronomist N. Borlaugh; sociobiologist W. Wilson; author I. Asimov; English professor Richard Adams; columnist Jack Anderson; Nobel physicist Murray Gell-Mann; basket ball player Wilt Chamberlain; columnist Ann Landers; her sister columnist "Dear Abby"; John W. Knowles, physician and head of the Rockefeller Foundation; John D. Rockefeller III; former secretary of HEW Robert Finch, and many others... Nobel Prize winners such as John Northrop, Linus Pauling and William Shockley have concurred in these ideas.

There is a striking difference between people beliefs about their own local situation and the situation in the U.S. of America as a whole. Opinion polls in the U.S. and the U.K. find that people do not find their neighborhoods over populated, but they think that their country is overpopulated.

Those who are convinced that overpopulation is an undisputable fact tend to use inflammatory terminology and "persuasion by epithet", as Julian Simon points out:

"Fear of population growth has been inflamed by extravagant language. Examples are the terms "population explosion," "people pollution," and "population bomb." These terms are not just the catchwords of population wordsmiths, whose rhetoric one is accustomed to discount. Rather, they have been coined by distinguished scientists and professors."

In particular, Paul Ehrlich said: *"We can no longer afford merely to treat the symptoms of the cancer of population growth; the cancer itself must be cut out"* (Paul R. Ehrlich, "The Population Bomb,"

New York, 1968). In his Nobel Peace Prize speech, Norman Bor-laugh spoke about "the population monster" and "the population octopus." As Julian Simon says:

"Bad terms drive out good. Reasoning by epithet may well be part of the cause of the fear of population growth in the U.S."

In the following, Simon discourses phony arguments, both crude and subtle, used by the birth control proponents:

"There are a number of specific ads in the campaigns (by Planned Parenthood) including one that was head lined "How Many Children Should You Have? Three? Two? One? Another adduced "Ten Reasons for Not Having children"; and, finally, the most offensive one was called the "Family Game"; the game was staged on a great monopoly word and every time the dice of life were thrown and a child was born... the background radio announced the disasters that came in the wake of children..."

Julian Simon shows that according to the birth control propagandists the contribution that children make to persons and to society is a purely negative one. All children are a loss, because they take space, constrict freedom and consume income which could be used otherwise. They can't see that children contribute to the happiness of their parents and their grandparents. And specially they do not see that in the future children may contribute ordinarily or extraordinarily to produce material, cultural, scientific and spiritual goods which may be a blessing for their family, their city, their country or the whole world. Simon goes on:

"Not all anti-natalist rhetoric is that subtle. Some of it is crude name-calling, especially the attacks on the Catholic church and on people with Catholic connections. An example is the bold black headline by the Campaign to Check the Population Explo-

sion: "Pope denounces birth control as millions starve"... Consider, for example, the religion-baiting of Colin Clark – a world-respected economist who presented data showing the positive effects of population growth- by sociologists Lincoln and Alice Day: "Colin Clark, an internationally known Roman Catholic economist and leading advocate of unchecked population growth..."

As Julian Simon points out, Gunnar Myrdal is not a Catholic and is a Nobel Prize winner, but he has called the concept of optimum population level a "most sterile idea." On the other hand, Paul Ehrlich and others refer to Clark as an "elderly Catholic economist." Everybody, if not dead prematurely, may become elderly, including Ehrlich, but not everybody has as many great professional achievements as Clark.

"Why is Population Rhetoric So Appealing?" Julian Simon asks himself. He does a good job giving a number of reasons for this, which we can briefly summarize by his own headlines:

- "Short-run costs are inevitable, whereas long-run benefits are hard to foresee."
- "Population causes pollutions"
- "Population exhausts natural resources"
- "Judgments about people's rationality: Other people will not act rationally in the face of environmental and resource needs"
- "Media exposure: Anti-natalist views get enormously more exposure than pro-natalist or neutral views"
- "Money: Population agencies have vast sums of money at their disposal –UNFPA and USAID- clearly see as their goal the reduction of population growth in the poorer countries"

And so on. Next Simon asks himself what are the underlying reasons for the dooms day fears and the rhetoric.

A summary of the reasons given by him follow:

- Simple world-saving humanitarianism

- Taxation fears

- Supposed economic and political national self-interests

- Fear of Communism

- Dislike of a business economy

- Belief in the superiority of "natural" processes

- Disturbance of the natural ecological order

- Religious antagonisms: Protestants have feared the growth of Catholics in the US, Hindus the growth of Muslims in India

- The belief that the more educated know best

- Lack of historical perspective

- (Eugenic) Preoccupation with the fitness of the human race based upon unproven genetic ideas

In other words disguised racist considerations.

In conclusion, Julian Simon, gives two "bottom line" propositions:

(1) *"U.S. tax money is being used to implement the aims of population activists and organizations…"*

(2) *"Though an important motivation of many of these people surely is the simple good-will desire to help people to go ahead… not absent from this movement (the population activists and organizations) are the beliefs that poor people… are inherently inferior"*

Of course, this brief summary does not do justice to the complete argumentation, more fully developed in the article in Human Life Review and in Julian Simon's book "The Rhetoric of Population Control" (Princeton University Press: Princeton, 1981).

Section 3

Rate Equations Approach and the Future of World Population

CHAPTER 10
USING A RATE EQUATIONS APPROACH TO MODEL WORLD POPULATION TRENDS[*]

by Julio A. Gonzalo and Felix F. Muñoz

Introduction

The UN data on world population, fertility rates, birth and death rates provide abundant and reliable information to investigate present population trends, and to make guesses about the future. These data can be complemented with vital statistical data from the UN Department of Economic and Social Affairs.[1]

In what follows we introduce population rate equations (Dekker, 1962; Loudon, 2000; Gonzalo et al., 2002) appropriate to describe the evolution of the population of a two level system in terms of the known birth rate $\left(BR=r_b\right)$ and death rate $\left(DR=r_d\right)$, under the assumption that total biomass is approximately conserved. Global biomass would play the role of a universal constant that somehow provides an upper limit to population, at least in the short-medium term. Obviously global biomass can change within certain limits depending on environmental conditions but it is not completely elastic. In this paper we use a rate equations approach (Gonzalo, 2010) to describe world population dynamics which involve a conservative

---

[*] Julio A. Gonzalo, Felix F. Muñoz and David Santos, *Simulation* (Transactions of The Society for Modeling and Simulation International), February 2013, Volume 89 Number 2.

principle. Within a human generation (about 25 years) the world total biomass may be expected to change at most a factor of 2 to 3 – except if a nuclear war, global pestilence or the collision of a comet with our planet take place.

The Earth has a biosphere capable of sustaining life: plants, animals and men. It has been estimated that the total amount of living matter on Earth is about 1.4×10^{15} Kg according to the World Atlas of Biodiversity (Groombridge and Jenkins, 2002).[2] Men, like other higher animals, live on a diet of carbohydrates, fats and proteins. As it is well known, in the last instance, the chain of life in our planet begins with photosynthesis by the green plants. According to FAO (see Vian Ortuño 1994) the distribution of vegetal biomass is roughly the following: 46% forests and lower wild vegetation; 10% pastures and steppes; 1.8% deserts; 6.2% crops; 2.9% biomass in continental waters; 33% biomass in the oceans. At present the ratio of human to total biomass is roughly

$$\frac{\text{Human Biomass}}{\text{Total Biomass}} \approx \frac{60 \times 6.8 \times 10^{9}}{1.4 \times 10^{15}} \approx 2.9 \times 10^{-4}$$

The consumption (and large-scale waste) of energy is of course an important factor affecting world population. However, it should be kept in mind that converting directly 1/6000 of the radiant energy coming from the Sun would provide sufficient electrical or chemical energy to satisfy present world energy needs. Fusion energy research may someday contribute effectively to provide abundant, safe and clean energy.

Under the above mentioned assumption, the solutions of rate equations are shown to simulate quantitatively well the actual time evolution of the world population $P(t)$ in the second part of the twentieth century, and to provide reasonable grounds for estimating quantitatively the short term evolution of world population. The main result of this paper is that a linear extrapolation of the actual data up to 2020 suggests a population decrease in the world at about mid-century. This result is consistent –at least partially- with UN, World Bank and IIASA projections for the rest of the century (assuming the medium scenario).[3]

As far as we know rate equations have not been previously used to determine world population trends. A main advantage of this approach is that it needs very few numerical parameters to simulate population trends in comparison to other alternative approaches.[4]

The paper is organized as follows: in section 2 we derive the rate equations that we use to describe and predict world population in the 21st Century; section 3 offers a brief analysis of World population data from 1950 to 2010; section 4 presents the results of applying rate equations to describe quantitatively world population trends; and finally, section 5 is the conclusion.

Rate equations

We consider a certain step change (up or down) in population associated with a correlative change (up or down) in human biomass $\Delta M (Kg)$ such that the final change in population (after the step is over) is given by

$$\Delta N \cong \Delta M (Kg) / 60 \, (Kg) = N_2(t) + N_1(t) \qquad (1a)^5$$

Where $N_2(t)$ is the number of individuals (men and women) actually alive at time t, and $N_1(t)$ the number of individuals potentially alive at the same time. $N_1(t)$ corresponds, therefore, to the amount of biomass potentially convertible into human mass at that time. Time t is in the interval (beginning) $t_i \leq t \leq t_f$ (end), where t_f is sufficiently larger than the relevant characteristic time τ^* for the step (up or down). We can assume ΔN to be in the range $10^9 < N < 10^{11}$, in principle, and N_{RL} (the background replacement level population at $t < t_i$) to be of the same order of magnitude.

During the transition between $N(0) = N_{RL}$ (original replacement level) to $N(t_f) = N_{RL} + \Delta N(t_f)$ (final replacement level) the excess human biomass is distributed between the two levels in such a way that always

$$N_2(t) + N_1(t) = \Delta N(t_f)$$

(1b)

At any given time there is a certain birth rate, $BR = r_b$, governing the transition of human biomass from level 1 to level 2, and a certain death rate, likewise governing the transition from level 2 to level 1.

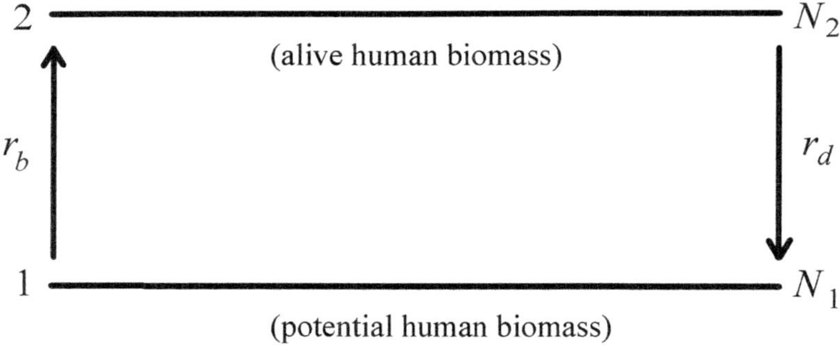

Figure 10.1. The world as two level system to describe step (+/-) over a certain population background (Replacement Level)

We can define the respective transition probabilities (say per 100 or 1000 persons) per unit time as

$$p_{12} = r_b = r_0 e^{\alpha} \quad \text{(birth rate)} \tag{2}$$

$$p_{21} = r_d = r_0 e^{-\alpha} \quad \text{(death rate)} \tag{3}$$

where $r_0 \equiv p_0 e^{-\alpha_0}$ could be viewed as the product of an attempt frequency p_0 (inverse of a natural characteristic time 2τ) modified by a reducing factor $e^{-\alpha_0} \leq 1$.

Alfa (α) in equations (2) and (3) can be taken as a kind of 'growth potential', determinant of the increase (or decrease) of population in the time interval considered. Then,

$$r_b \times r_d = r_0^2 = (1/2\tau)^2 \text{, hence } 1/\tau = (r_b \times r_d)^{1/2} \tag{4}$$

$$r_b/r_d = e^{2\alpha} \text{, hence } \alpha \equiv \frac{1}{2}\ln(r_b/r_d) \tag{5}$$

The population rate equation can be written therefore as

$$\frac{dN_2}{dt} = N_1 p_{12} - N_2 p_{21} \tag{6}$$

$$\frac{dN_1}{dt} = -N_1 p_{12} + N_2 p_{21} \tag{7}$$

Subtracting Eq. (7) from Eq. (6) we get

$$\frac{d(N_2 - N_1)}{dt} = (N_2 + N_1)(p_{12} - p_{21}) - (N_2 - N_1)(p_{12} + p_{21}) \tag{8}$$

which, taking into account that $[N_2(t) - N_1(t)] = \Delta P(t)$ is the increase in live population at time t, and $[N_2 + N_1] = \Delta N$ (constant), can be rewritten as

$$\frac{d\Delta P}{dt} = N 2 r_0 \sinh\alpha - \Delta P 2 r_0 \cosh\alpha \tag{9}$$

Using $p(t) = \Delta P(t)/N$, dimensionless, Eq. (9) becomes

$$\frac{dp(t)}{dt} = \frac{1}{\tau}\left[\sinh\alpha - p(t)\cosh\alpha\right] \tag{10}$$

The general solution of this linear differential equation (see Kreyszing, 1972) is

$$p(t) = e^{-\int(\cosh\alpha/\tau)dt}\left[\frac{\sinh\alpha}{\tau}e^{\int(\cosh\alpha/\tau)dt}dt + C\right] \tag{11}$$

In particular, for a step (up or down) in growth potential, say from $\alpha=0$ at $t=0$ to $\alpha\neq0$ at $t>0$, the integrals in Eq. (11) are straight-forward, and we get

$$p(t) = e^{-(\cosh\alpha/\tau)dt}\left[\tanh\alpha\times e^{(\cosh\alpha/\tau)dt} + C\right] \tag{12}$$

which, from $p(0)=0$ at $t=0$ leads to

$$C = -\tanh\alpha \tag{13}$$

resulting in

$$p(t) = \tanh\alpha\left[1 - e^{-(\cosh\alpha/\tau)dt}\right] \tag{14}$$

Therefore, using $p(t)\equiv\Delta P(t)/N$ we finally get

$$P(t) = P_{RL} + \Delta P_{max}\tanh\alpha\left[1 - e^{-(t-t_i)/\tau^*}\right] \tag{15}$$

where $\tau^* = \tau / \cosh \alpha$, for a step up ($\alpha > 0$) in population.

Eq. (15) describes a step up in population due to an increase in fertility rate, a decrease in death rate (life expectancy increase) or a combination of both resulting in a net growth rate. The starting growth population level -occurring at time t_i- is denoted by P_{RL}. We note that only two numerical parameters (in addition to P_{RL}) are needed to describe the time evolution of the whole set of World population data for such the step up: the population growth potential α (related to the ratio of birth rate to death rate, as given in Eq. (5)) and τ^* (related to the product of the same rates as given in Eq. (4)).

As will be seen below, the model works: it fits well the set of UN data from 1950 to 2010 and suggests a declining future trend for the world population based upon UN data for 2000-2010. The rate equation model has the definite advantage of reflecting recent past changes in birth rates and death rates, which are determinants of the 'momentum' of world population evolution.

Analysis of world population data (1950-2010)

In order to analyze in detail the available UN world population data (1950-2050), and to make some qualitative considerations about future trends, it is convenient first to introduce an empirical relationship between the birth rate $(BR = r_b)$, defined as the number of births per year per 100 population, and the fertility rate (FR), defined as the average total number of children per woman.

Fig. 10.2 gives the data for birth rate vs. fertility rate for China, India, USA and Russia (1995-2010) summarized in Table 10.1. The relationship

$$(BR) = 0.72(FR) \times 10^{-2} \tag{16}$$

is very approximately fulfilled. Here the proportionality factor between (BR) and (FR) has been slightly corrected to take into account that the global female to male population in those countries is about. (% female)/(% male) $\cong$ 0.935.

Table 10.1. Birth rate and fertility rate for various countries (1995-2010)

Year	China BR	China FR	India BR	India FR	USA BR	USA FR	Russia BR	Russia FR
1995	1.82	2.3	2.93	3.9	1.57	2	1.07	1.6
2000	1.62	1.8	2.59	3.2	1.47	2	0.93	1.4
2005	1.3	1.7	2.33	2.9	1.41	2.1	0.96	1.3
2010	1.24	1.7	2.23	2.8	1.4	2.1	1.05	1.4

Source: UN.

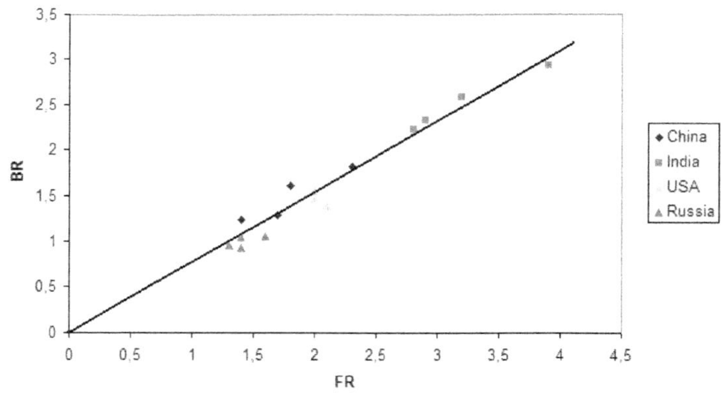

Figure 10.2. Birth rate per 100 population versus Fertility rate for China, India, USA and Russia (1995-2010). An excellent correlation is found by means of $(BR) = (0.72)(FR) \times 10^{-2}$

Source: www.unpopulation.org

UN data for world fertility rates (FR) and the world growth rates (GR) for 1950-2010 are available at United Nations web, from which the birth rate ($BR = 0.72 \times FR$) and the death rate ($DR = BR - GR$) are directly obtained. The corresponding numbers for growth potential $\alpha = \ln(BR / DR)/2$ and inverse characteristic time $1/\tau = 2(BR \times DR)^{1/2} \times 10^{-2}$ are given in subsequent columns. Projected UN rates for subsequent years are given for completeness. It can be seen that, in spite of the fact that (BR) and (DR) vary considerably with time between 1950 and 2000, the numerical values for $x = BR / DR \approx 2.57$ and $\alpha = \ln(BR / DR)/2 \approx 0.471$ can be used as representative values for the half century through which a large step up in population is taking place. The numerical value for τ, however, varies smoothly from about $\tau = 18.4$ years in 1950 to about $\tau = 40.18$ years in 2000. This can be correlated to the increase in life expectancy and possibly to a marked delay in the life-giving age for women. (Table 10.2 gives in the first two columns the UN world fertility rates (FR) and the world growth rate (GR) for 1950-2010, from which the birth rate $BR = 0.72 \times FR$ and the death rate $DR = BR - GR$ are directly obtained.)

Table 10.2. UN demographic data (1950-2010) and projections (2010-2040)

Year	FR (UN)	GR (UN)	BR (Eq.16)	DR (Eq.17)	x BR/DR	α Eq.5	τ^{-1} Eq.4	τ^{*} $\tau / \cosh \alpha$
1950	5.02	1.80	3.61	1.81	1.99	0.345	0.0512	18.42
1960	4.97	1.97	3.58	1.61	2.22	0.400	0.0480	19.28
1970	4.48	1.94	3.23	1.29	2.51	0.460	0.0407	22.17
1980	3.57	1.71	2.57	0.86	2.99	0.547	0.0297	29.15
1990	3.03	1.50	2.18	0.68	3.20	0.582	0.0244	34.93
2000	2.48	1.07	1.79	0.72	2.50	0.457	0.0226	39.98
2005	2.22	0.87	1.60	0.73	2.19	0.393	0.0216	42.98
2010	2.05	0.74	1.48	0.74	2.01	0.348	0.0208	45.21

Table 10.2. (Cont'd)

2020	1.87	0.48	1.35	0.87	1.55	0.220	0.0216	45.19
2030	1.71	0.17	1.23	1.06	1.16	0.074	0.0229	43.62
2040	1.59	0.10	1.14	1.04	1.10	0.046	0.0219	45.67

Using the data from the Population Division of the UN Department of Economic and Social Affairs we may analyze in detail the *step up* in world population taking place between 1950 and 2010, and then, taking into account that x (and α) begin to decrease in the year 2000, we can guess on the time for the incipient *step down* in world population.

Results

In Fig. 10.3, the normalized population $p(t) = \tanh \alpha \left[1 - e^{t/\tau^*} \right]$, $\tau^* = \tau / \cosh \alpha$, is given as a function of t/τ^* for various values of $x = r_b / r_d$, ($\alpha = 1/2 \ln x$). It can be seen that a replacement level (*RL*) is achieved in all cases for $t/\tau^* > 3$, and that the population at the replacement level grows in proportion to $\tanh \alpha$.

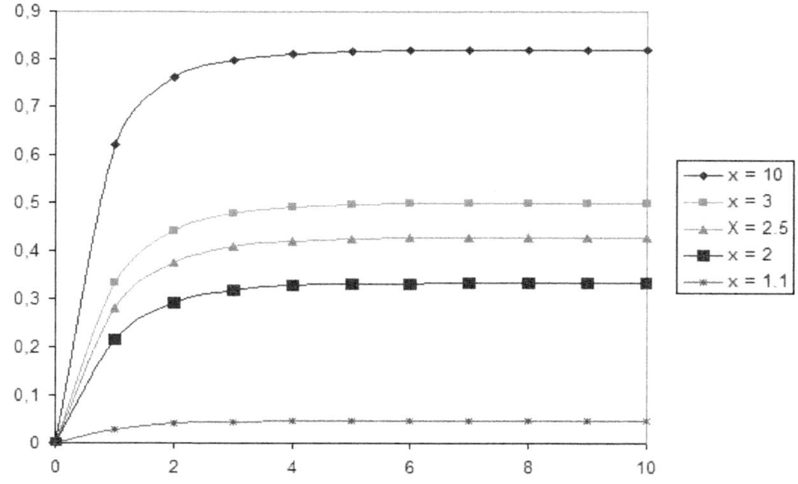

Figure 10.3. Normalized population increase versus normalized time

for various $x = r_b / r_d$ .Curves: $p(t) = \tanh\alpha\left[1 - \exp(-t / \tau^*)\right]$; $\tau^* \approx \tau / \cosh\alpha$.

(For different values of $x = r_b / r_d$, $\alpha = \ln x / 2$.)

Figure 10.4 gives the birth rate (*BR*) and the death rate (*DR*) per year per 100 population as a function of time: actual UN data (1950-2010), UN (2004) projections for the period 2010-2050 are also given. It is seen that, in the interval (1950-2000), *BR* and *DR* decrease monotonously and smoothly, keeping the ratio (*BR*)/(*DR*) approximately constant. In the interval 2000-2010 a change in *DR* is taking place, probably related to the fact that in some countries, like Japan, the transient surplus population connected with the sustained increase in life expectancy, accompanied by the decrease in effective fertility rate, is beginning to fade away. During this interval the world population still increases slowly but it is leveling out. There is no such a thing as an exponential increase.

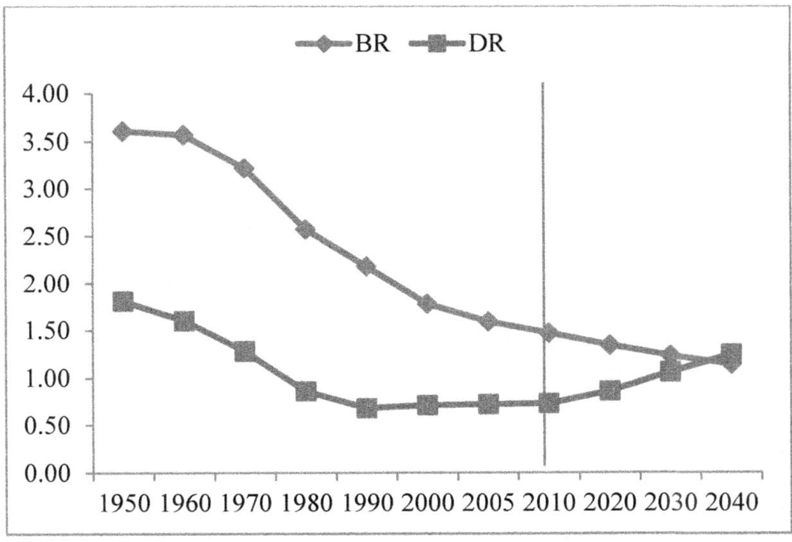

Figure 10.4. Birth rate ($\times 10^2$) and death rate ($\times 10^2$) UN actual data (1950-2010) and UN projections (2010-2050). See Table 10.2

Figure 10.5 displays the *population growth potential* α (dimensionless) and the *characteristic time* τ (years) in the same time span. α remains practically constant up to $t = 2000$, and then begins to drop up to 2010. A linear extrapolation of the actual data for $\alpha(t)$ up to 2020 suggests a population decrease at about mid-century. On the other hand τ evolves smoothly from $\tau(1950) \approx 18.4$ years to $\tau(2000) \approx 40.2$ years and then begins to change tendency.

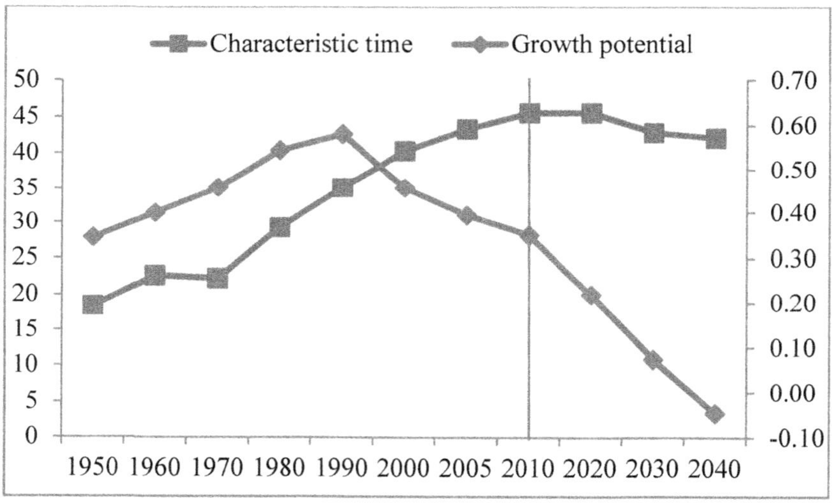

Figure 10.5. Growth potential (α) and characteristic time (τ): UN actual data (1950-2010) and UN projections (2010-2050). See Table 10.2

If the characteristic time reflects a global tendency for women to have children at later ages (which might well be the case), by the year 2000, this age may be approaching already the age at which women become infertile. For the period 1950-2000 we can take an average value $\tau \approx 30.3$ years which would result in an effective $\tau^* = \tau / \cosh \alpha \approx 27.2$ years for the above period.

Finally Fig. 10.6 gives the actual UN data (and the 2004 projections) and the theoretical curves describing the time evolution of the world population (1950-...). The Malthusian projection[6] for population growth beyond 1980 is also given for comparison: $P(t) = P(t_0)(2)^{(t-t_0)/25}$ with $P(1980) = 4.5 \times 10^9$ at $t_0 = 1980$.

The analysis presented in this work could suggest further research in the factors influencing birth rates in women and men, as well as death rates. Regarding birth rates, of course there is a maximum number of children a woman wish or is able to have. Also regarding death rates there is a maximum which human nature is made to live.

Table 10.3. Population step amplitude in the period 1975-2010

t	1975	1980	1985	1990	1995	2000	2005	2010
$t - t_i$	10	15	20	25	30	35	40	45
$\Delta P_m \tanh \alpha$	8.2	7.1	7.0	6.8	7.5	8.1	8.2	8.5

The step amplitude is obtained directly from the UN data for $P(t)$, $P_{RL} = 1.6$ and $\tau^*(t)$ for $t_i = 1965$ using:

$$\Delta P_{max} \tanh \alpha \equiv \left[P(t) - P_{RL} \right] / \left[1 - e^{-(t-t_i)/\tau^*} \right];$$ we take $\tau \sim \tau^*$ from Table 10.2.

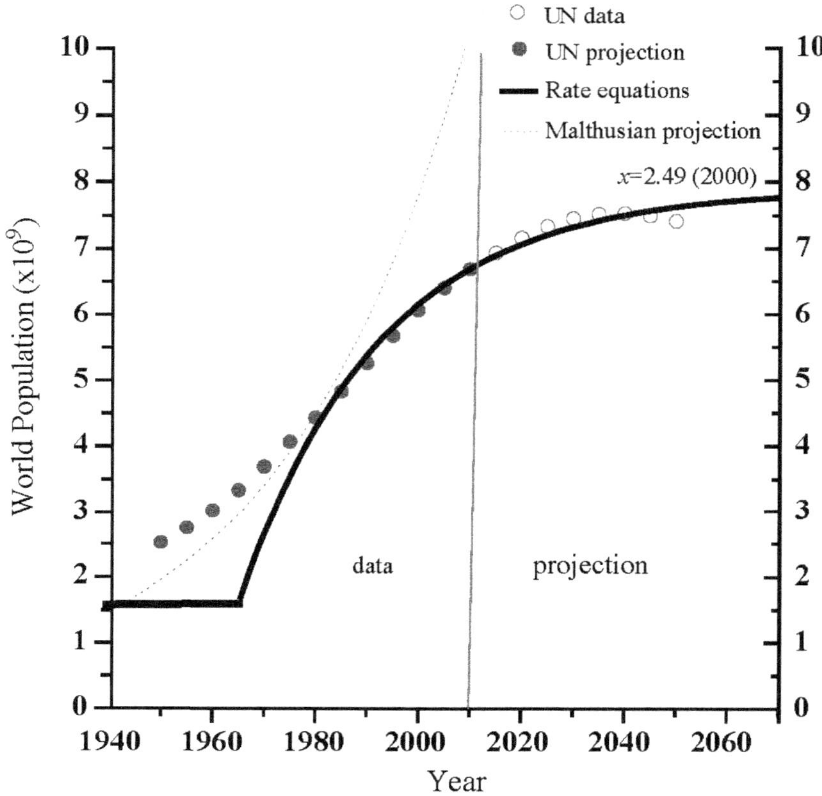

Figure 10.6. World population $P(t)$ versus time. 1950-2010: UN data (red circles); Rate equations (continuous curve) 2010-2050: UN projections (white circles)

Concluding remarks

Our analysis of world population data by means of Eq. (15) fits the UN data satisfactorily and shows clearly that the population increase in 1950-2010 should be attributed more to the transient decrease in death rate level (related to the increase in life expectancy) than to nonexistent increase in birth rate, which was decreasing consistently already even before the 1950's, even before chemical contraceptives and legalized abortion begun to play any role.

An exponential population growth can be discarded as totally unrealistic at least at the next half century. Using fitting parameters extracted from recent UN population data, our rate equation solutions approach, which indicates that $x(t)=r_b(t)/r_d(t)$ may approach to one at $t\sim2032\pm10$, suggests a decrease in world population beginning to take place about this time.

In 1960 population and world economic development was examined in *Science*. At about the same time, Foerster, Mora and Amiot (1960) reported in *Science* that that November 13th, 2026 would be the date at which world population would become infinity. The prediction was based upon an empirical equation for the population with a denominator going to zero as time increases. Today, 2011, world population is approaching 7.0×10^9 and, according to the UN data it will be around 7.3×10^9 in the year 2026 and approaching a maximum somewhat later.[7] (Reports in Science on the UN Conferences on World Population at Bucharest and Mexico were given by Boersma (1975) and Lutz, O'Neill and Scherbov (2003).)

The evidence for 'negative momentum' in Europe's population around 2000 is a result of low fertility rates. Caldwell (2008) most recently, criticizes Mathew Connelly's book 'Fatal Misconceptions. The Struggle to Control World Population'. Eberstadt (1997; 2001), on the other hand, points out that the world today may confront an unfamiliar crisis: rapidly decreasing birthrates and declining life spans that might set back the progress of human developments. Work by other authors share this perspective (see for instance Chaunu 1997; Ulrich 2000; Yea 2004).

The UN Press Release reports world population figures for 2050 and 2100, *if* fertility in all countries converge to replacement levels. Total fertility for the world and for countries grouped by fertility level in 1965-1970, 2005-2010, 2045-2050 and 2095-2100 are given. It may be noted that a large decrease between 4.8 and 2.5 is recorded for 1965-70/2005-10, much larger than the (expected) low decrease between 2.2 and 2.0 for 2045-50/2095-2100.

We think a rate equation approach is validated by the good fit of Eq. (15) to the UN data involving only two fitting parameters may provide a useful tool to simulate world population trends for the near future.

REFERENCES

[1] Population Division. http://www.un.org/esa/population/unpop.htm

[2] Asimov (1972: 795) gives a figure of 2×10^{16} Kg.

[3] They differ only by the speed of decrease for fertility. For more details see Leridon (2008).

[4] The partially similar approach has been developed by Miranda and Lima (2010; 2011). These authors employ logistic and power law methodologies for both retrospective and prospective analyses of extended time series describing evolutionary growth processes, in environments with finite resources. Their projections for world population are consistent with ours.

[5] We have estimated roughly the weigth per person as 60 ± 15 Kg. In any case this estimation does not change the general argument.

[6] As it is well known, T.R. Malthus held that "population, when unchecked, increases in geometric proportion ... doubling itself every twenty five years..." (Malthus, 1985[1798], Chp. I –II).

[7] The lower most likely estimate: The 2004 Revision/ The 2010 Revision. See esa.un.org/wpp/Documentations.htm (accessed March 26th, 2012).

FURTHER READING

Asimov, I. *Asimov's Guide to Science*. New York: Basic Books, 1972.

Boersma, D. "World Population Conference in Perspective." *Science* 188, no. 4193 (1975): 1069-69.

Caldwell, J.C. "Fatal Misconception - the Struggle to Control World Population." *Science* 321, no. 5892 (Aug 2008): 1043-43.

Chaunu, P. "From Explosion to Implosion of the Population - Vital Peril." *Cahiers d'Economie et Sociologie Rurales* 181, no. 9 (Dec 1997): 1923-33.

Dekker, A.J. *Solid State Physics*. Englewood Cliffs, NJ: Prentice Hall, 1962.

Eberstadt, N. "The Population Implosion." *Foreign Policy*, no. 123 (Mar-Apr 2001): 42-53.

"World Population Implosion?" *Public Interest*, no. 129 (Fal 1997): 3-22.

Foester, H v; Mora, P.M. and Amiot, L.W. "Doomsday: Friday, 13 November, A.D. 2026." *Science* 132 (1960): 1291.

Gonzalo, J.A. "On the usefulness of the hyperbolic functions to describe physical phenomena". *Ferroelectrics* 401 (2010): 9-16.

Gonzalo, J.A., Frutos, J. and Garcia, J. *Solid State Spectroscopies*. Singapore: World Scientific, 2002.

Groombridge, B., and Jenkins M.D. *World Atlas of Biodiversity. Prepared by the Unep World Conservation Monitoring Centre*. Berkeley, USA: University of California Press, 2002.

Kreyszing, E. *Advanced Engineering Mathematics*. New York: Wiley, 8th edition, 1998.

Leridon, H. "Human populations and climate: Lessons from the past and future scenarios." *Geoscience* 340 (2008): 663-669.

Loudon, R. *The Quantunm Theory of Light*. Oxford: Oxford Science Publication, 2000.

Lutz, W., B. C. O'Neill, and S. Scherbov. "Demographics: Europe's Population at a Turning Point." *Science* 299, no. 5615 (Mar 2003): 1991-92.

Lutz, W., Sanderson, W. and Scherbov, S. "The end of world population growth." *Nature* 412, (Aug 2001): 543-545.

Malthus, T.R. *Essay on the Principle of Population as it Affects The Future Improvement of Society*. London: Penguin Classics, 1985 [1798].

Miranda, L.C.M. and Lima, C.A.S. "On the logistic modeling and forecasting of evolutionary processes: Application to human population dynamics." *Technological Forecasting and Social Change*, 77(5) (2010): 699-711.

Miranda, L.C.M. and Lima, C.A.S. "On the forecasting of the challenging world future scenarios." *Technological Forecasting and Social Change*, 78(8) (2011): 1445-1470.

Ulrich, R.E. "Explosion of the World Population or Implosion?" *Internationale Politik* 55, no. 12 (Dec 2000): 17-24.

Vian Ortuño, A., ed. *Introducción a La Química Industrial*. Barcelona: Editorial Reverte, 1994.

Yea, S. "Are We Prepared for World Population Implosion?" *Futures* 36, no. 5 (Jun 2004): 583-601.

CHAPTER 11
PROSPECTS OF WORLD POPULATION SLOW DOWN[*]
by Julio A. Gonzalo and Felix F. Muñoz

In Science (4 November 1960) Friday 13 November AD 2026 was given as the "Doomsday" of planet Earth, a doomsday produced by "world population" going to infinity. In that paper, a rudimentary rate equation describing the evolution of world population with time was approximated in such a way that a quantitative calculation resulted in that "doomsday." In this paper, we give a more realistic rate equation respecting general conservation principles and compare previous results and the results of our calculation with actual UN data for 1960-2010 and UN medium term projections. At present there is disagreement among experts as to what is to be expected for world population in the years to come: some think population is still growing out control, some of them say it will be approximating a constant level about 2050 and others expect it to be in clear decline between 2050 and the end of 21st century. Our model shows that if no drastic and unexpected change takes place worldwide soon, world population will be slowing down at an accelerated pace after 2050. Our rate equation approach is similar to that used in condensed matter physics and chemical physics to describe the evolution of a two level system under an external perturbation and the results is much more realistic than a purely exponential result as generally assumed in the last decades of last century.

---

[*] Gonzalo, J.A., Muñoz, F.F., 2014. *Prospects of world population decline in the near future: a short note.* Departamento de Análisis Económico, U.A.M.

Introduction

'Doomsday: Friday, 13 November, A.D. 2026.' This was the original title of an article published in *Science* (4 November 1960) by Heinz von Foester, Patricia M. Mora and Lawrence W. Amiot.[1] They warned in the article's subtitle that at this date human population will approach infinity if it grows as it has grown in the last two millennia. Von Foester et al. begin arguing that in any biological system the time evolution of the total population is determined by two factors: fertility and mortality, and that the rate of change should be given by

$$\frac{dN}{dt} = \gamma_0 N - \theta_0 N = \alpha_0 N \tag{1}$$

where $\alpha_0 = \gamma_0 - \theta_0$ may be called the 'productivity'. This equation results, of course, for $\alpha_0 = \text{constant}$, in an exponential (Malthusian) increase for any $\alpha_0 > 0$. The authors then consider the case of 'hypothetical paradise' in which no environmental hazards, no limited food supply and no detrimental interactions between the individual members of the population need to be taken into consideration. This is, of course, not very realistic, and they proceed to relax the assumption of $\alpha_0 = \text{constant}$ and, somewhat arbitrarily, they assume the productivity α changing as a function of N as

$$\alpha = \alpha_0 N^{1/k} \tag{2}$$

where α_0 and K can be fitted to the available experimental data for human population in an extended time interval. Their approach leads to

$$N(t) = K\big/(t_0 - t)^n \qquad\qquad (3)$$

where k, t_0 and n are adjusted to the available world population data. k has the meaning of a population number at $(t_0 - t) = 1$ measured (arbitrarily) in years, t_0 is the so called 'doomsday time' and n is a dimensionless exponent that, using their chosen set of data, comes out close to one. Obviously, Eq. (3) blows up at $t = t_0$ for any $n > 0$.

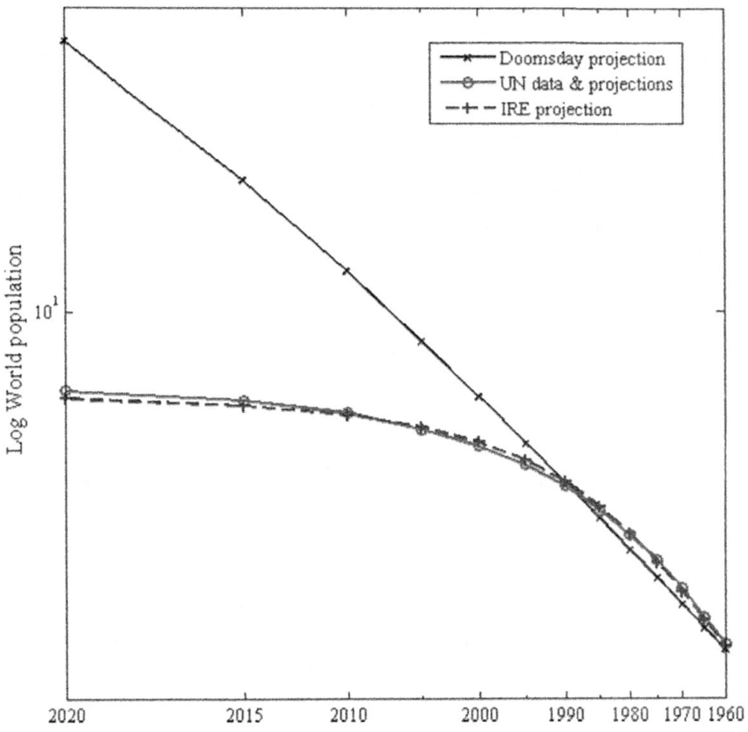

Figure 11.1. World population trends

This is, of course, very unphysical. The total mass upon the Earth surface is strictly conserved. It cannot grow, and much less grow to infinity. The total biomass can grow somewhat, but always within definite limits. Further, von Foester et al. estimate K, t_0 and n for the human world population as $K = 1.79 \times 10^{11}$, $t_0 = 2026.87 \pm 5.5$ years (which can be approximated as 2026), and $n = 0.99$. Using these data in Eq. (3), it implies that $N(1960) = 2.82 \times 10^9$ -somewhat lower that the UN estimate for that year, $N_{UN}(1960) \simeq 3.02 \times 10^9$. Using $K = 1.91 \times 10^{11}$ instead of $K = 1.79 \times 10^{11}$, takes care of the difference.

Figure 11.1 gives, in the same log-log representation used by von Foester et al. ($\log_{10} N(t)$ vs. $\log_{10}\left(k/(t_0 - t)\right)$, i.e. the time evolution of total world population from well before 1960 to some years beyond 2010. It is seen that the UN data fall well upon the 'doomsday' curve from 1960 to 1990 but begins to deviate substantially thereafter. By 2010, $\left[P(t)\right]_{vF}$ as estimated by von Foester et al., is about 444 times larger than the actual $\left[P(t)\right]_{UN}$ value for that year.

In the final paragraph of their paper, the authors point out that among the suggestions made to solve the problem of the incoming of the world population explosion, legislation, heavy taxation of families with more than two children, tax deduction cancellations, etc., and even *space travel* had been proposed recently.[2] But, they add, no re-entry permit to Earth can be given to those flying away from our planet.

About forty years later Wolfgang Lutz, Sanderson, and Scherbov (2001), published 'The end of world population growth' in *Nature*, in which they conclude that this growth is likely to come to an end in the foreseeable future. They improve on earlier methods of probabilistic forecasting and show that there is around an 85 per cent chance that the world's population stops growing before the end of the century, a 60 per cent chance that it will not exceed 10 billion people before 2100, and some 15 per cent that it will be less at the end of the century that at its beginning.

They conclude also that there is a 20 per cent chance that a peak of population would be reached by 2050. As we will see below, using an 'improved rate equations' (*IRE*) model, and the additional actual world population data for 2001-2013, we conclude that a maximum (not a peak) in world population around 2045 is likely with a likelihood substantially higher than 20 per cent. The decrease in population from the maximum value around 7.75 billion in 2045, will be likely to around 7.66 billion in 2090, with a substantial decrease of 90 million.

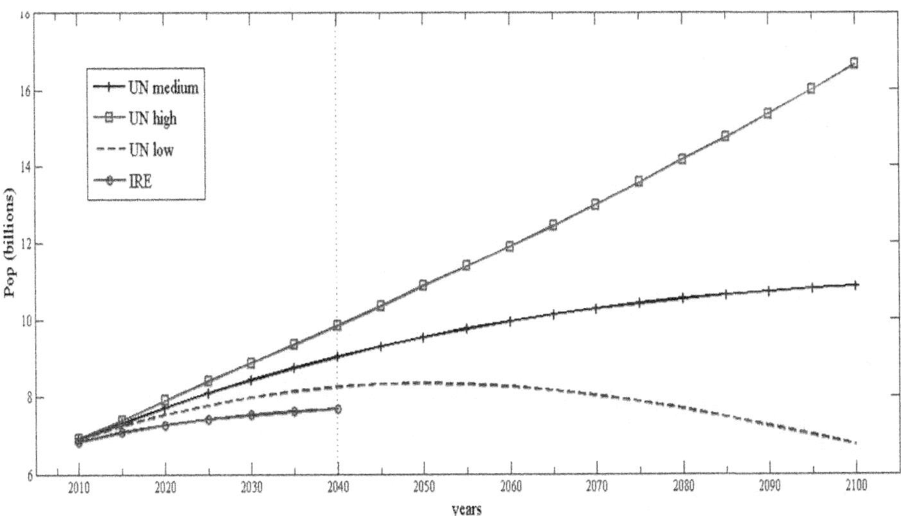

Figure 11.2. UN and IRE projections

Figure 11.2 gives the estimated total world population in billions for the years 2000-2100 as given for the high, medium, and low fertility variant UN scenarios. The actual data for 2000-2010 (black circles) and the IRE projections (see below) for 2000-2040 (open circles) are also given. It may be seen that the low UN scenario fits better than the medium UN scenario the actual data for 2000-2010 and is closer to the IRE projection for 2000-2040.

Lutz et al. examine also regional population trends and conclude that the extent of the regional differences in the speed of population ageing, concomitant with population stabilization and decline, will pose major social and economic challenges. They conclude that the prospect of an end to population growth is welcome news for efforts towards a sustainable development, but this conclusion is far from substantiated for the time being as the recent global economic crisis clearly suggests. They say also that the main determinant of the timing of the 'pick' in population size is the assumed speed of fertility decline in the past of the world that still have relatively higher fertility. However, it may be noted that the spectacular increase in world population in the second half of the 20th century was due mainly to a sustained increase in *life expectancy* rather than to an increase in fertility, which did not ceased to go down from the early fifties onwards.

An improved rate equations approach

Recently, Gonzalo et al. (2013) proposed a novel rate equations approach to modelling world population trends. This approach is designed to describe *steps* up or down in population in a *two level system* (individuals in level (2) *alive*; individuals in level (1) *dead* or *potentially alive* in the relative abundant available biomass). The rate equations are:

$$\frac{dN_2}{dt} = N_1 p_{12} - N_2 p_{21} \tag{4}$$

$$\frac{dN_1}{dt} = -N_1 p_{12} + N_2 p_{21} \tag{5}$$

resulting in

$$\frac{d(N_2 - N_1)}{dt} = (N_1 + N_2)(p_{12} - p_{21}) - (N_2 - N_1)(p_{12} + p_{21}) \tag{6}$$

where $(N_1 + N_2) = N$ is related to the maximum jump in population, $\Delta P_{max} \times (N_2 - N_1)$ is related to the actual change in population $\Delta P(t)$ at time t, at which $N_2 = N_2(t)$ and $N_1 = N_1(t)$, and p_{12} is directly related to the birth rate (r_b), and p_{21} to the death rate (r_d). Two important dynamic parameters, $\alpha = \frac{1}{2} \mathrm{Ln}\,(r_b/r_d)$ (dimensionless) and $\tau = (r_b \cdot r_d)^{-\frac{1}{2}}$ (a dimension of time) are defined. A general solution of Eq. (6) leads to

$$P(t) = P_{RL} + \left[\Delta P_{max} \cdot \tanh \alpha\right]\left[1 - e^{-(t-t_i)/\tau}\right] \tag{7}$$

P_{RL} is the population at replacement level before the jump, t_i is the inflection time for a jump in population (we are considering here a jump up) and τ^* is a characteristic time, obviously related to the effective fertility time span in the women population making up always about one half of the total human population.

Eq. (7) can be conveniently rewritten[3] taking into account that for a well defined jump in population $P(t)$ first grows gradually from P_{RL} towards $P_{RL} + \frac{1}{2}[\Delta P_{max} \cdot \tanh \alpha]$ and then grows gradually from this population to $P_{RL} + [\Delta P_{max} \cdot \tanh \alpha]$, as given by

$$P(t) = P_{RL} + \frac{1}{2}[\Delta P_{max} \cdot \tanh \alpha]\left[1 + \tanh \frac{t - t_i^*}{\tau^*}\right] \qquad (8)$$

A good fit to the UN data is obtained with $P_{RL} = 2$ billion, $\Delta P_{max} \cdot \tanh \alpha = 2.93$ billion, $t_i^* = 1985$ and $\tau^* = 30$ years. This is what we have called the improved rate equations (*IRE*) solution for our model, describing in this case the time evolution of world population for a population jump up.

Projections and discussion

Before using Eq. (8) to analyse population data and to make momentum-like projections for the near future, let us investigate the trend of the annual relative increase in world population $\delta P(t)/P(t)$ (per cent per year) as a function of time. Figure 11.3 gives the actual UN population increase rate for 1950-2010 for 2004 and the revised UN population increased rate for 2013 as well as the increase rate obtained using Eq. (8).

It can be seen that extrapolating linearly from 1990 forward the UN data, $\delta P(t)/P(t)$ becomes zero about $t = 2045 \pm 16$. At this time world population must go through a transient maximum of about 7.75 billion. Thereafter if the birth rate continues to decrease, and the death rate (concomitant with a decrease in the average life expectancy due to overall ageing of the population as a whole) decreases also, the overall decrease in world population becomes something to be anticipated.

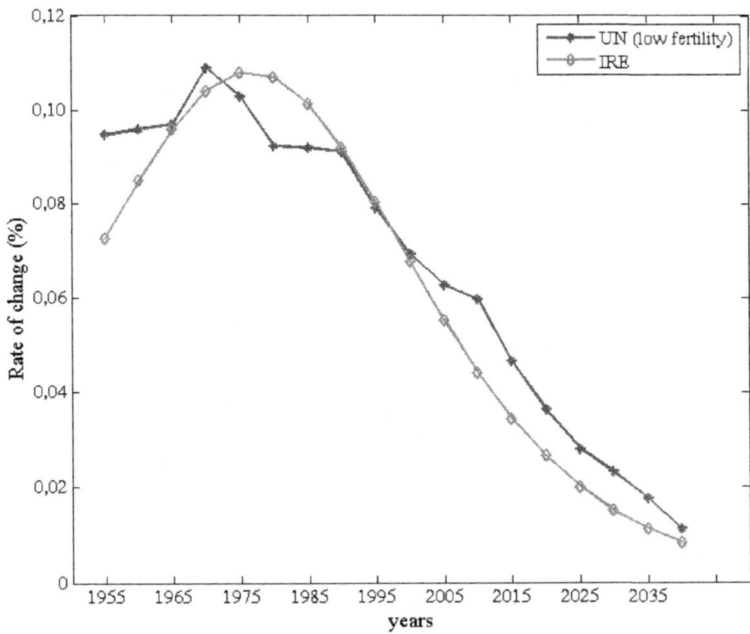

Figure 11.3. Rates of change of population: UN & IRE

Finally, we give in Figure 11.4 the UN world population data (black circles) for 1950-2010 and the world population projections obtained by means of Eq. (8), the IRE solution (open circles), for 2020-2045. We can see that the IRE solution fits very well the data. We show also in this graph that UN estimation projections for the world population in 2010 made in the period from 1990 to 1998 where substantially larger than the actual value at 2010, with the estimates decreasing gradually as they approached 2010. The UN overestimations of future world population for 2020 and 2030 in previous decades seem to be negligible if $P(t)$ calculated using Eq. (8) is correct.

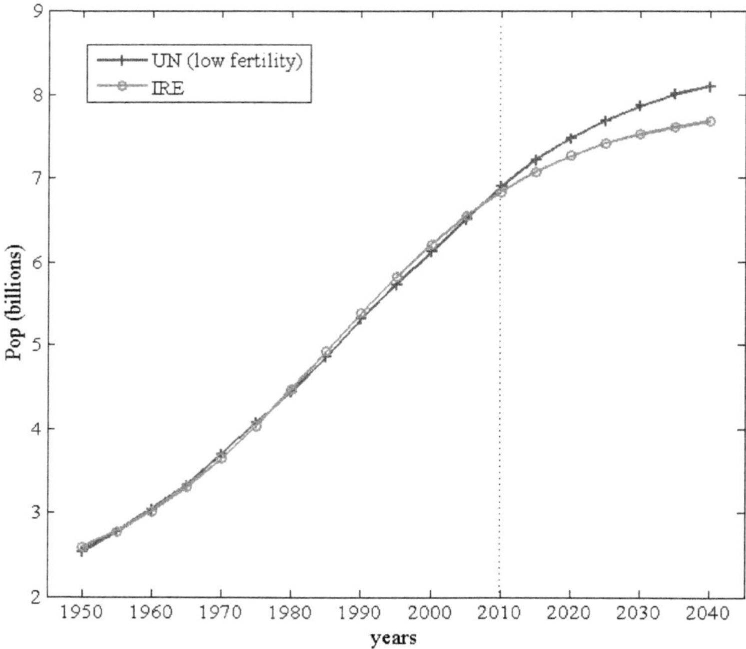

Figure 11.4. UN & IRE projections

Concluding remarks

Of course, no statistical model can predict changes in global socio-cultural trends, such as global increases in casualties of epidemics, or such as the rise or fall of world hegemony, like the Soviet Union in the past or perhaps China or the U.S. of America in the future, or such as European legislation leading to massive contraception (or possible reversals in these politics), as well as possible changes in demographic trends, favouring a voluntary fertility rate compatible with a slow increase in population. But in the short and medium term projections based upon our *IRE* model, which take properly into account the role of momentum, may be used to demand attention about the incoming slow down (and eventually decline) population in the second half of this century, and may prepare the ground among economists, sociologists, and politicians to face the inevitable consequences.

REFERENCES

[1] Foester, H. v., Mora, P. M., & Amiot, L. W. (1960). Doomsday: Friday, 13 November, A.D. 2026. *Science, 132,* 1291

[2] Christopher, R. C., & Griffith, T. (1960). Time, 75, 22.

[3] Gonzalo, J. A., Muñoz, F.-F., & Santos, D. J. (2013). Using a rate equations approach to model World population trends. Simulation: Transactions of the Society for Modeling and Simulation International, 89(2), 192-198. doi: 10.1177/0037549712463736

CHAPTER 12
FALLING BIRTH RATES AND WORLD POPULATION PROJECTIONS: A QUANTITATIVE DISCUSSION (1950-2050)[*]

by Felix F. Muñoz and Julio A. Gonzalo

The UN data (1950-2010) and projections (both medium and low-fertility variants for 2015-2050) show that birth rates are already below replacement level in all continents except Africa. In this chapter, we develop a simple approach for population projections based on an Improved Rate Equations (*IRE*) model. Population projections under the (1) Malthusian assumption, (2) an IRE model fitting and extrapolating from actual UN population data up to 2050, and (3) UN projections (both medium and low-fertility variant), are compared. The model fits quite well actual data and suggests a world population stagnation in the 21st Century. The economic, social and political consequences of this new and global

Introduction

Although demography is a determining factor in explaining the long-term development of an economy -together with 'the stock of

---

[*] Muñoz, F.F., Gonzalo, J.A., 2013. *Falling birth rates and world population decline 1950-2040*. Departamento de Análisis Económico, U.A.M.

human knowledge particularly as applied to the human command over nature; and the institutional framework that defines the deliberate incentive structure of a society' (North, 2005: 1; Sachs, 2002), it is usually understated in economic growth theory. Population long-term dynamics is often described in a very simplified way by means of simple dynamic models. For example, in economic growth literature, economic growth models usually assume that labor (as an approximation for population) increases following the rule $L_t = L_0 e^{nt}$, with $L_0, n > 0$ (see Acemoglu, 2009). This is a typical Malthusian (1985 [1798]) dynamics partially assumed by UN projections.[1]

In this chapter, we present a quantitative discussion of world population prospects which questions Malthusian dynamics. Extrapolating UN data (available since 1950), it would be expected that world population stagnates by middle 21st century because of the sharp decline in birth rates presently observable both globally and by continents. According to the population database of the Population Division of the Department of Economic and Social Affairs of the UN Secretariat,[2] fertility rates are below replacement levels in all continents except (by the moment) Africa.[3] Because of the momentum gained in previous decades, world population and continental population in Africa, the Americas (Northern America and Latin America), Asia and Europe are still increasing at a slow rate, but demographers see signs of decrease in world population somewhere around the middle of the 21st century (Chaunu, 1997; Eberstadt, 2001).

The implications of the expected evolution of population are far reaching from an economic point of view –and indeed from *any* point of view: social, political, geo-strategic, environmental, urban policy, etc. (Ulrich, 2000; Yea, 2004; *The Economist*, 2015). And this not only because of population stagnation but to a great extent to the change in the age composition of human population. For the first time in history humanity as a whole confronts ageing as a global problem.

In order to simulate world population trends, we present in this chapter a simple mathematical model using a hyperbolic tangent solution fitting effectively any jump in population level. This is an Improved Rate Equation (*IRE*) approach to model population dynamics.[4] Other main contribution consists of applying this *IRE* to the world as a whole.[5] Previously, a rather similar rate equations approach has been proposed by the authors to describe steps up or down in population due to changes in Birth Rate (*BR*), Death Rate (*DR*), or both (see Gonzalo et al., 2013). In this kind of models, a step up in population between a given starting population level (at replacement level) $\left(P_{RL}\right)_n$ and a certain *final* population level $\left(P_{RL}\right)_{n+1}$, -where P means 'population', RL 'replacement level' and n and $n + 1$ refer, respectively, to the initial level and to the final level for which population dynamics evolves at a certain rate.[6] In our previous models, population dynamics was determined by BR and DR. Suppose a given replacement level, that would correspond to a fertility rate about 2.1 and $BR \simeq DR$. Since the UN data show that the overall fertility (world and individual continents except Africa) has decreased consistently in the period 1950-2010 (see Nations, 2014), we assume that the long-term initial $\left(DR\right)_n$ -compensated for a $\left(BR\right)_n \simeq \left(DR\right)_n$ - is higher than the final $\left(DR\right)_{n+1}$ -compensated for a $\left(BR\right)_{n+1} < \left(BR\right)_n$ in the long run. Under these assumptions, population dynamics is essentially governed by an increase in life expectancy (*LE*). However, increases in life expectancy cannot go on forever: it is only a transitory state.[7]

The structure of the chapter is as follows. Section 2 is devoted to population data analysis both globally and by continents; this section also shows and compares the projections of world population of

UN and those obtained with the *IRE* model. The main prediction of *IRE* model is that world population will stagnate by mid-21st century. Section 3 discusses the main findings and implications of this population trend.

Data analysis, trends and projections

UN data (1950-2010) show a strong proportionality between the birth rate (*BR*) and fertility rate (*FR*). Table 12.1 shows how consistent is the proportionality between *BR* and *FR* for the world and the various continents, Africa included.[8]

Table 12.1. Birth rates over fertility rates by continents and the world

Africa	0.7114
Europe	0.7502
Asia	0.7267
Northern America	0.7205
Latin America	0.7334
World	**0.7394**

From birth rate and death rate data we define and compute the following variables $x = BR/DR$, $y = BR \cdot DR$, $\alpha = 1/2 \log x$, $\tau^{-1} = 2y^{1/2} \cdot 10^{-2}$ and τ (characteristic time) for the years 1950-55 to 2005-2010, adding the extrapolated UN data –using UN medium-fertility variant hypothesis- for the period 2015-2050.[9] In all cases, the raw UN data are Crude Birth Rate and Crude Death Rate per 1,000 population. Table 12.2 shows these data and calculations for Africa, Asia, Europe, Northern America, Latin America, Oceania and the World respectively.

Table 12.2. Regional and world population data: 1950-2050
Source: UN World Population Prospects: The 2012 Revision (accessed June 2015). For 2015-2050 we use the medium-fertility variant 2010-2100

Table 12.2a. Africa

years	BR	DR	x	y	α	τ^{-1}	τ
1950-55	47.735	26.783	1.782	12.785	0.289	0.072	13.984
1955-60	47.656	24.341	1.958	11.600	0.336	0.068	14.681
1960-65	47.361	22.223	2.131	10.525	0.378	0.065	15.412
1965-70	46.578	20.388	2.285	9.496	0.413	0.062	16.225
1970-75	46.123	18.719	2.464	8.634	0.451	0.059	17.016
1975-80	45.478	17.111	2.658	7.782	0.489	0.056	17.924
1980-85	44.328	15.677	2.828	6.949	0.520	0.053	18.967
1985-90	42.527	14.618	2.909	6.217	0.534	0.050	20.054
1990-95	40.209	14.358	2.800	5.773	0.515	0.048	20.809
1995-00	38.370	13.821	2.776	5.303	0.511	0.046	21.712
2000-05	37.133	13.197	2.814	4.900	0.517	0.044	22.587
2005-10	35.587	11.762	3.026	4.186	0.554	0.041	24.439
2010-15	34.039	10.446	3.259	3.556	0.591	0.038	26.516
2015-20	32.299	9.594	3.367	3.099	0.607	0.035	28.404
2020-25	30.280	8.882	3.409	2.689	0.613	0.033	30.489
2025-30	28.518	8.270	3.448	2.358	0.619	0.031	32.558
2030-35	27.012	7.767	3.478	2.098	0.623	0.029	34.520
2035-40	25.663	7.373	3.481	1.892	0.624	0.028	36.349
2040-45	24.355	7.078	3.441	1.724	0.618	0.026	38.082
2045-50	23.060	6.879	3.352	1.586	0.605	0.025	39.699

Table 12.2b. Asia

years	BR	DR	x	y	α	τ^{-1}	τ
1950-55	41.803	22.624	1.848	9.458	0.307	0.062	16.259
1955-60	39.246	20.239	1.939	7.943	0.331	0.056	17.741
1960-65	38.507	18.872	2.040	7.267	0.357	0.054	18.548

Table 12.2b. (Cont'd)

years	BR	DR	x	y	α	τ^{-1}	τ
1965-70	38.131	13.268	2.874	5.059	0.528	0.045	22.229
1970-75	34.551	11.265	3.067	3.892	0.560	0.039	25.344
1975-80	29.629	9.894	2.995	2.931	0.548	0.034	29.203
1980-85	28.785	9.138	3.150	2.630	0.574	0.032	30.829
1985-90	28.023	8.539	3.282	2.393	0.594	0.031	32.323
1990-95	24.808	7.989	3.105	1.982	0.567	0.028	35.516
1995-00	22.035	7.600	2.899	1.675	0.532	0.026	38.637
2000-05	19.761	7.078	2.792	1.399	0.513	0.024	42.278
2005-10	18.611	6.998	2.659	1.302	0.489	0.023	43.813
2010-15	17.484	7.141	2.448	1.249	0.448	0.022	44.748
2015-20	16.179	7.288	2.220	1.179	0.399	0.022	46.046
2020-25	14.976	7.578	1.976	1.135	0.341	0.021	46.935
2025-30	13.995	8.022	1.745	1.123	0.278	0.021	47.189
2030-35	13.247	8.602	1.540	1.140	0.216	0.021	46.839
2035-40	12.661	9.261	1.367	1.173	0.156	0.022	46.175
2040-45	12.153	9.924	1.225	1.206	0.101	0.022	45.529
2045-50	11.697	10.555	1.108	1.235	0.051	0.022	44.999

Table 12.2c. Europe

years	BR	DR	x	y	α	τ^{-1}	τ
1950-55	21.442	11.161	1.921	2.393	0.326	0.031	32.321
1955-60	20.723	10.183	2.035	2.110	0.355	0.029	34.420
1960-65	19.077	9.704	1.966	1.851	0.338	0.027	36.748
1965-70	16.716	9.891	1.690	1.653	0.262	0.026	38.885
1970-75	15.588	10.179	1.531	1.587	0.213	0.025	39.694
1975-80	14.757	10.510	1.404	1.551	0.170	0.025	40.149
1980-85	14.339	10.787	1.329	1.547	0.142	0.025	40.203
1985-90	13.704	10.647	1.287	1.459	0.126	0.024	41.394
1990-95	11.510	11.246	1.023	1.294	0.012	0.023	43.947

Table 12.2c. (Cont'd)

years	BR	DR	x	y	α	τ^{-1}	τ
1995-00	10.238	11.547	0.887	1.182	-0.060	0.022	45.986
2000-05	10.153	11.636	0.873	1.181	-0.068	0.022	46.001
2005-10	10.757	11.289	0.953	1.214	-0.024	0.022	45.373
2010-15	10.840	11.625	0.932	1.260	-0.035	0.022	44.541
2015-20	10.573	11.819	0.895	1.250	-0.056	0.022	44.728
2020-25	10.149	11.960	0.849	1.214	-0.082	0.022	45.383
2025-30	9.827	12.170	0.807	1.196	-0.107	0.022	45.721
2030-35	9.855	12.508	0.788	1.233	-0.119	0.022	45.035
2035-40	10.182	12.923	0.788	1.316	-0.119	0.023	43.588
2040-45	10.480	13.296	0.788	1.393	-0.119	0.024	42.357
2045-50	10.575	13.558	0.780	1.434	-0.124	0.024	41.757

Table 12.2d. Northern America

years	BR	DR	x	y	α	τ^{-1}	τ
1950-55	24.570	9.549	2.57	2.35	0.47	0.03	32.64
1955-60	24.560	9.300	2.64	2.28	0.49	0.03	33.08
1960-65	22.029	9.295	2.37	2.05	0.43	0.03	34.94
1965-70	17.743	9.351	1.90	1.66	0.32	0.03	38.82
1970-75	15.714	9.187	1.71	1.44	0.27	0.02	41.61
1975-80	15.070	8.616	1.75	1.30	0.28	0.02	43.88
1980-85	15.435	8.539	1.81	1.32	0.30	0.02	43.55
1985-90	15.514	8.647	1.79	1.34	0.29	0.02	43.17
1990-95	15.116	8.528	1.77	1.29	0.29	0.02	44.04
1995-00	13.902	8.462	1.64	1.18	0.25	0.02	46.10
2000-05	13.747	8.392	1.64	1.15	0.25	0.02	46.55
2005-10	13.702	8.084	1.69	1.11	0.26	0.02	47.51
2010-15	13.477	8.188	1.65	1.10	0.25	0.02	47.60
2015-20	13.304	8.304	1.60	1.10	0.24	0.02	47.57
2020-25	13.036	8.474	1.54	1.10	0.22	0.02	47.57

Table 12.2d. (Cont'd)

years	BR	DR	x	y	α	τ^{-1}	τ
2025-30	12.732	8.782	1.45	1.12	0.19	0.02	47.29
2030-35	12.618	9.254	1.36	1.17	0.16	0.02	46.27
2035-40	12.654	9.773	1.29	1.24	0.13	0.02	44.96
2040-45	12.665	10.179	1.24	1.29	0.11	0.02	44.04
2045-50	12.612	10.356	1.22	1.31	0.10	0.02	43.75

Table 12.2e. Latin America

years	BR	DR	x	y	α	τ^{-1}	τ
1950-55	42.663	15.529	2.747	6.625	0.505	0.051	19.426
1955-60	41.929	13.694	3.062	5.742	0.560	0.048	20.866
1960-65	41.112	12.233	3.361	5.029	0.606	0.045	22.296
1965-70	37.814	10.940	3.456	4.137	0.620	0.041	24.583
1970-75	35.127	9.742	3.606	3.422	0.641	0.037	27.029
1975-80	32.976	8.672	3.803	2.860	0.668	0.034	29.567
1980-85	30.692	7.825	3.922	2.402	0.683	0.031	32.264
1985-90	27.888	7.064	3.948	1.970	0.687	0.028	35.623
1990-95	25.326	6.531	3.878	1.654	0.678	0.026	38.877
1995-00	23.173	6.142	3.773	1.423	0.664	0.024	41.911
2000-05	21.425	5.963	3.593	1.278	0.639	0.023	44.236
2005-10	19.286	5.887	3.276	1.135	0.593	0.021	46.925
2010-15	17.819	5.904	3.018	1.052	0.552	0.021	48.748
2015-20	16.483	6.009	2.743	0.990	0.505	0.020	50.240
2020-25	15.269	6.193	2.466	0.946	0.451	0.019	51.418
2025-30	14.155	6.447	2.196	0.913	0.393	0.019	52.340
2030-35	13.206	6.788	1.945	0.896	0.333	0.019	52.810
2035-40	12.438	7.220	1.723	0.898	0.272	0.019	52.763
2040-45	11.829	7.729	1.530	0.914	0.213	0.019	52.292
2045-50	11.340	8.294	1.367	0.941	0.156	0.019	51.556

Table 12.2f. World

years	BR	DR	x	y	α	τ^{-1}	τ
1950-55	36.858	19.141	1.926	7.055	0.33	0.053	18.824
1955-60	35.412	17.315	2.045	6.132	0.36	0.050	20.192
1960-65	34.617	16.226	2.133	5.617	0.38	0.047	21.097
1965-70	33.631	12.897	2.608	4.337	0.48	0.042	24.008
1970-75	31.319	11.574	2.706	3.625	0.50	0.038	26.262
1975-80	28.296	10.572	2.677	2.991	0.49	0.035	28.909
1980-85	27.712	9.961	2.782	2.760	0.51	0.033	30.094
1985-90	26.984	9.420	2.865	2.542	0.53	0.032	31.361
1990-95	24.466	9.095	2.690	2.225	0.49	0.030	33.519
1995-00	22.36	8.803	2.540	1.968	0.47	0.028	35.638
2000-05	20.847	8.408	2.479	1.753	0.45	0.026	37.766
2005-10	20.007	8.116	2.465	1.624	0.45	0.025	39.238
2010-15	19.150	8.061	2.376	1.544	0.43	0.025	40.243
2015-20	18.124	8.054	2.250	1.460	0.41	0.024	41.384
2020-25	17.089	8.141	2.099	1.391	0.37	0.024	42.391
2025-30	16.228	8.338	1.946	1.353	0.33	0.023	42.984
2030-35	15.590	8.640	1.804	1.347	0.30	0.023	43.081
2035-40	15.109	9.001	1.679	1.360	0.26	0.023	42.875
2040-45	14.675	9.358	1.568	1.373	0.22	0.023	42.667
2045-50	14.243	9.680	1.471	1.379	0.19	0.023	42.583

Figure 12.1 is a representation of (BR) vs. (FR), for the Europe and Northern America (1a), Africa and Latin America (1b), and Asia and the World (1c). The patterns are very similar and a quick reduction of the relationship between (BR) and (FR) is observed in all continents.

Figures 12.2a and 12.2b show the behavior of $x(t)$ and $\tau(t)$ respectively.[10] This last variable, characteristic time, can be correlated to the increase in life expectancy and possibly to a marked delay in the childbearing age of women. This characteristic time runs from a minimum of 13.9 (Africa, 1950-55) to a maximum of 52.8 (projection for Latin America, 2030-35) with an average (estimated) value of 37.2 for the whole period.[11] Time evolution of $x(t)$ and $\tau(t)$ by continents speak for themselves. The most interesting finding is that $\tau(t)$ tends to converge in all continents by 2050.

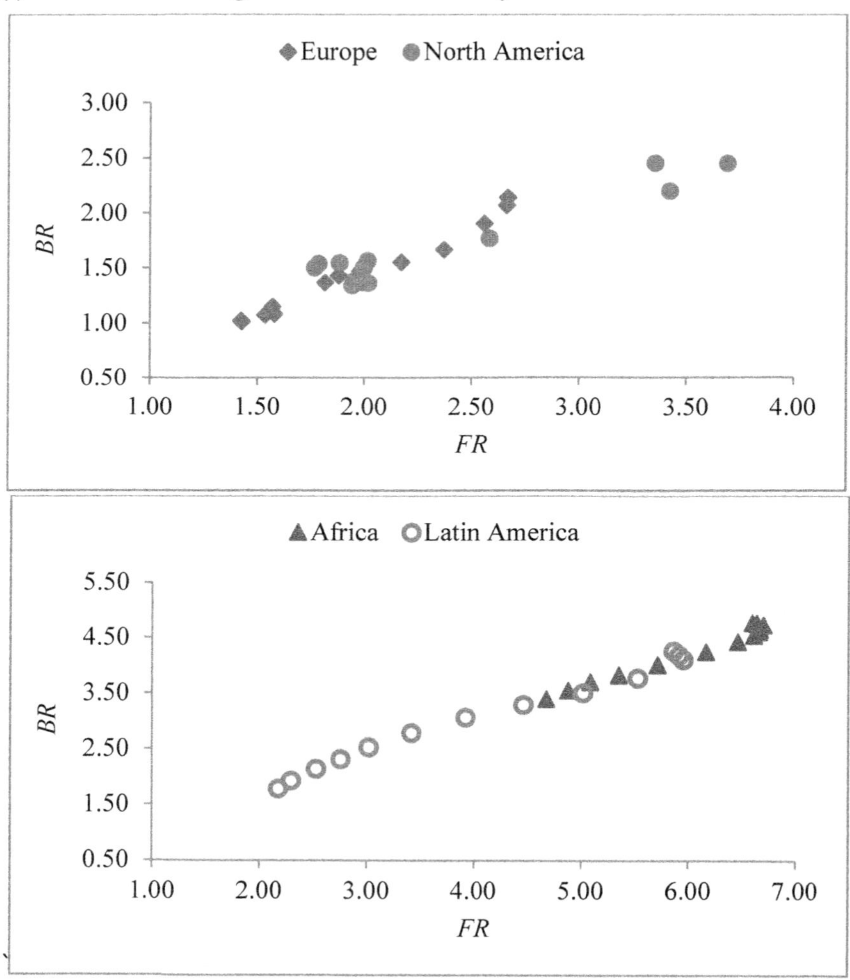

Figure 12.1. Birth rates (BR) versus Fertility Rates (FR) by continents and the world (1950-2010)

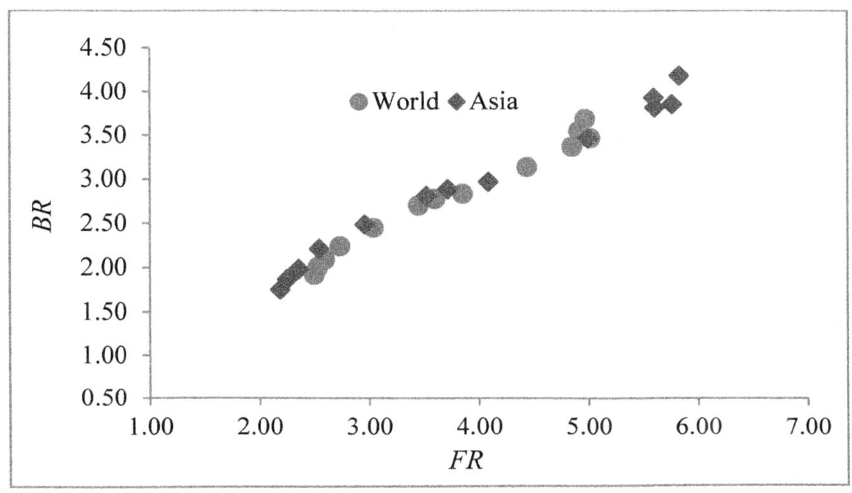

Figure 12.1. (Cont'd)

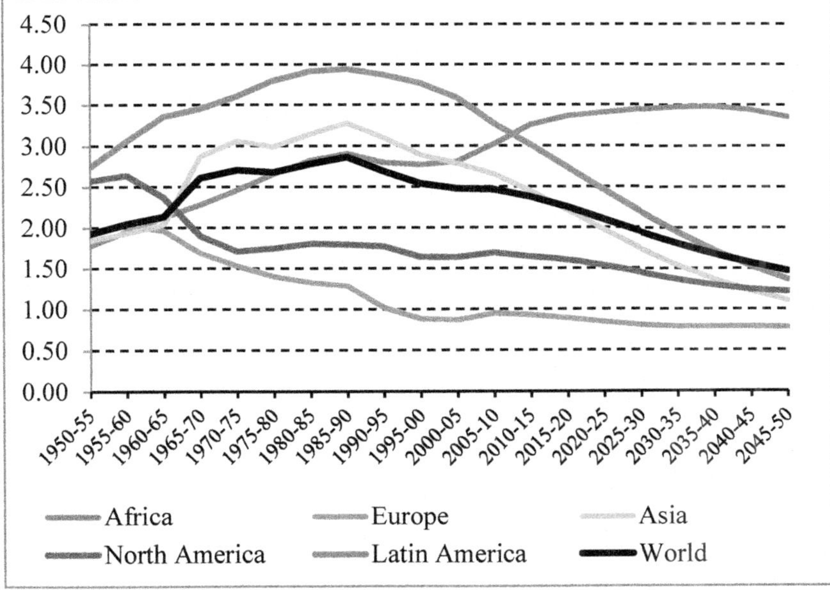

Figure 12.2a. $x(t)$

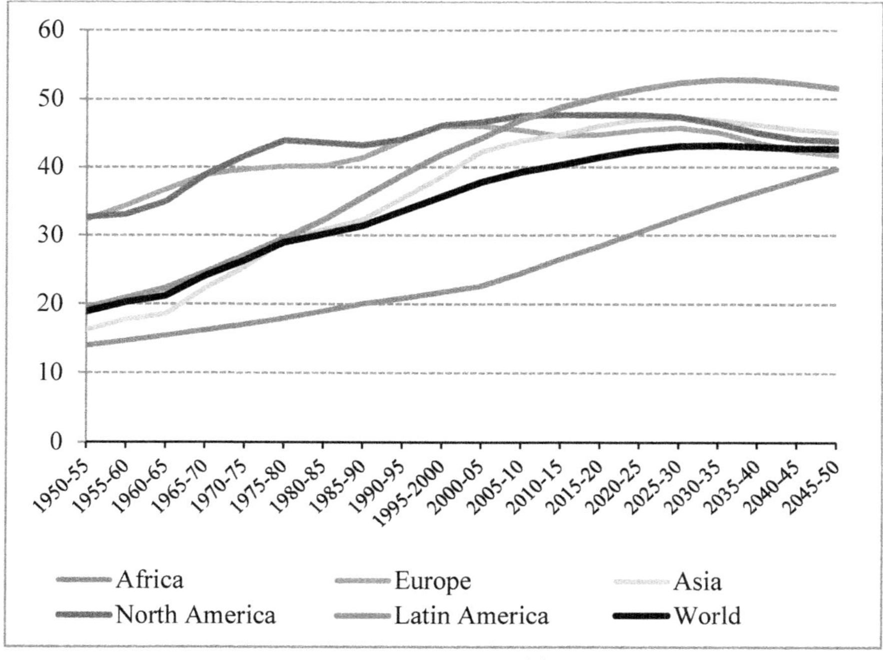

Figure 12.2b. $\tau(t)$

Source: UN and own elaboration.

Table 12.3 shows the world population (UN data) $P_{UN}(t)$ for the period 1950-2050, along with the calculated population using the *IRE* model $P_{IRE}(t)$, and a extrapolation of a Malthusian model.

In the case of the *IRE* model, population is projected by using the following expression:[12]

$$P_{IRE}(t) = P_{RL} + \frac{1}{2}\Delta P_m (\tanh \alpha)\left(1 + \tanh \frac{t - t_{inf}}{\tau^*}\right) \tag{1}$$

where $\Delta P_m (\tanh\alpha)$, t_{inf} and τ^* represent, respectively the jump amplitude, that depends on the values of $(RL)_n$ and $(RL)_{n+1}$ (in this case 5.86 billions), the inflection point (at year 1985), and the characteristic time.[13]

Table 12.3. World population 1950-2050: A comparison of Malthusian, (IRE) and UN projections

	1950	1955	1960	1965	1970	1975	1980	1985	1990	1995	2000
Pop(t) $_{UN}$	2.5	2.8	3.0	3.3	3.7	4.1	4.5	4.9	5.3	5.7	6.1
Pop(t) $_{IRE}$	2.6	2.8	3.0	3.3	3.6	4.0	4.5	4.9	5.4	5.8	6.2
Pop(t) $_{Malthus}$	2.5	2.8	3.0	3.3	3.7	4.1	4.5	4.9	5.3	5.8	6.4

	2005	2010	2015	2020	2025	2030	2035	2040	2045	2050
Pop(t) $_{UN}$	6.5	6.9	7.2	7.5	7.7	7.9	8.0	8.1	8.1	8.1
Pop(t) $_{IRE}$	6.6	6.8	7.1	7.3	7.4	7.5	7.6	7.7	7.7	7.8
Pop(t) $_{Malthus}$	6.9	7.6	8.3	9.1	9.9	10.9	11.9	13.0	14.2	15.5

Calculated population (P_{cal} using Eq. (1)) and UN data (P_{UN}). Fitting parameters $(t \geq 1985)$: $P_{\!_{RL}}(1960) \simeq 2.0 \times 10^9$; $t_{\text{inf}} = 1985$; $\tau^* \simeq \tau / \cosh\alpha = 30$ years; $1/2 \Delta P_m \tanh\alpha = 2.93 \times 10^9$.
Data source: World Population Prospects. The 2010 Revision. UN, New York, (low variant).
Data source: World Population Prospects. The 2010 Revision. UN, New York, (low variant), and for IRE, own calculations.

In order to fit the function to current UN data (for 1950-2010) and compute the associated projection, we use $P_{RL}(1960) \simeq 2.0 \times 10^9$, $t_{\text{inf}} = 1985$ and $\tau^* = 30$ years. Additionally, Eq. (1) makes use of the following approximation:

$$\frac{1}{2}(1 + \tanh x) \simeq \frac{1}{2}\left(1 + \left(1 - 2e^{-2x} + e^{-4x}\right)\right) = e^{-2\tau x}\left(1 - e^{-2(x - \delta x)}\right) \quad (2)$$

where $e^{-2\tau x} \equiv \left(1+\dfrac{1}{2}e^{-4x}\right)$ for x in the interval $0 \leq x \leq \infty$. This is equivalent to the previous (more abrupt) rate equation solution (Gonzalo et al., 2013) where $t_{inf} = 1965$ (instead of $t_{inf} = 1985$) and $\tau^* = 27.2$ years (instead of $\tau^* = 30$ years).

Figure 12.3 shows the good fit obtained for the time span 1950-2050.

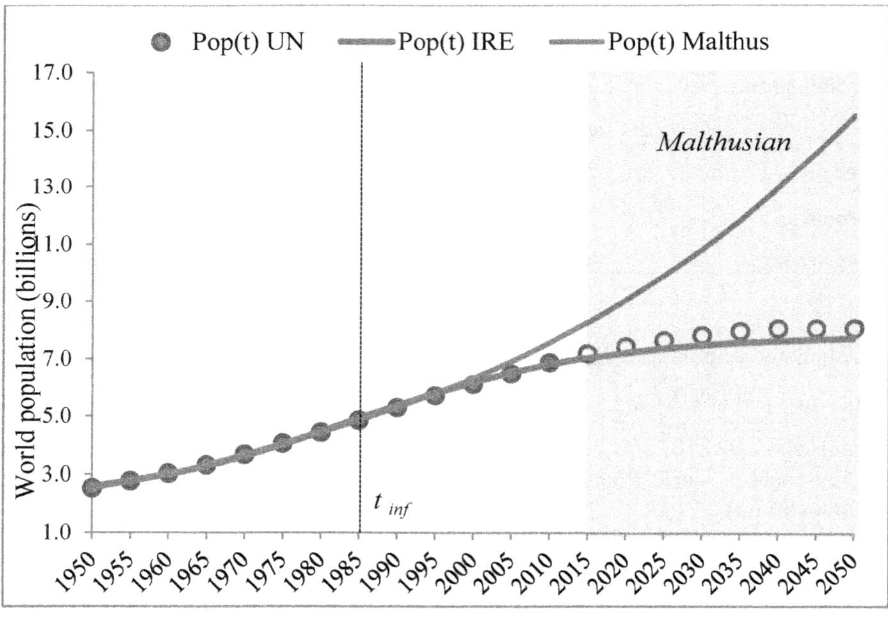

Figure 12.3. World actual (UN data), Malthusian and *IRE* population fit for the period 1950-2050

Note: The shadow area corresponds to projections.

Source: UN data and (IRE) model projection –Eq. (1).

$1/2\Delta P_m(\tanh\alpha) = 2.93$, $\tau = 32$, $t_{inf} = 1985$, $P_{RL} = 2.0$.

Table 12.4 gives in parallel columns the death rates and the estimated inverse female life expectancy of females $\left(LE_f\right)^{-1}$ for Africa, Europe, Asia, the Americas, and the World (1950-2010) extrapolated from actual data. There seems to be a minimum inverse life expectancy around $\left(LE_f\right)^{-1} = 1.2 \times 10^{-2}$ which corresponds to a maximum $\left(LE_f\right) = 83.3$ years. The world data follow a straight line going through the origin. (A zero death rate (*DR*) should correspond to an 'infinite life expectancy'.) The data for Europe seem to undergo a time reversal at about $\left(LE_f\right)^{-1} = 1.20 \times 10^{-2}$.[14] Data in Table 12.4, corresponding to 1950-2010, are depicted in Figure 12.4.[15]

Table 12.4. (*DR*) vs. $\left(LE_f\right)^{-1}$

Years	World		Africa		Europe		Asia		N. Amer.		L. Amer.	
	DR	*Lf-1*	*DR*	*Lf-1*	*DR*	*Lf-1*	*DR*	*Lf-1*	*DR*	*Lf-1*	*DR*	*Lf-1*
1950-55	1.871	0.021	2.710	0.025	1.073	0.015	2.570	0.023	1.130	0.014	2.380	0.019
1955-60	1.714	0.020	3.210	0.024	1.073	0.014	2.350	0.022	1.320	0.014	2.378	0.018
1960-65	1.612	0.019	3.260	0.023	1.041	0.014	2.120	0.021	1.130	0.014	2.357	0.017
1965-70	1.296	0.017	3.140	0.022	1.150	0.014	1.950	0.018	1.010	0.013	2.173	0.016
1970-75	1.175	0.017	2.880	0.021	1.080	0.013	1.640	0.017	1.140	0.013	1.849	0.016
1975-80	1.064	0.016	2.570	0.020	1.030	0.013	1.330	0.016	0.470	0.013	1.509	0.015
1980-85	1.010	0.016	2.390	0.019	1.060	0.013	0.960	0.016	0.470	0.013	1.230	0.015
1985-90	0.955	0.015	2.180	0.019	0.970	0.013	0.760	0.015	0.530	0.013	0.997	0.014
1990-95	0.925	0.015	1.810	0.019	1.065	0.013	0.690	0.015	0.860	0.013	0.852	0.014
1995-00	0.897	0.015	1.910	0.019	1.080	0.013	0.679	0.015	0.850	0.013	0.764	0.014
2000-05	0.869	0.015	1.760	0.018	1.140	0.013	0.694	0.014	0.880	0.013	0.728	0.013
2005-10	0.839	0.014	1.150	0.018	1.180	0.013	0.683	0.014	0.840	0.012	0.718	0.013

Source: World Population Prospects. The 2010 Revision. UN, New York.

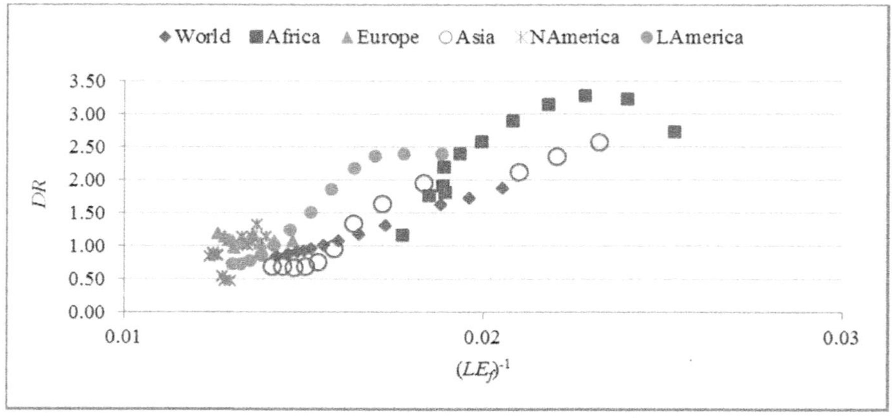

Figure 12.4. (DR) vs. $\left(LE_f\right)^{-1}$

Source: UN and own elaboration.

A comparison between the time evolution of Birth Rates and Death Rates for Europe and the World is given in Table 12.5 from 1950 to 2050.[16] The behavior of BR (related to the fertility rate) determine the trend of the population evolution in both cases. The *momentum* in the net growth rate due to normal fertility in previous generations does not show yet an actual decrease with time in the resulting net population for the world (BR is still larger than DR). But for Europe, after a long period of increasing 'life expectation', the death rate is already going up, and since about 2000, it has surpassed the declining birth rate ($EDR > EBR$).[17] Sometime around the middle of this century the same thing is likely to happen for the world as a whole. This is illustrated in Figure 12.5.

Table 12.5: Birth rates and death rates in Europe and the world

Year	Europe		World	
	(BR)	(DR)	(BR)	(DR)
1950-55	2.14	1.12	3.69	1.91
1955-60	2.07	1.02	3.54	1.73
1960-65	1.91	0.97	3.46	1.62

Table 12.5. (Cont'd)

Year	Europe		World	
	(BR)	*(DR)*	*(BR)*	*(DR)*
1965-70	1.67	0.99	3.36	1.29
1970-75	1.56	1.02	3.13	1.16
1975-80	1.48	1.05	2.83	1.06
1980-85	1.43	1.08	2.77	1.00
1985-90	1.37	1.06	2.70	0.94
1990-95	1.15	1.12	2.45	0.91
1995-2000	1.02	1.15	2.24	0.88
2000-05	1.02	1.16	2.08	0.84
2005-10	1.08	1.13	2.00	0.81
2010-15	1.08	1.16	1.92	0.81
2015-20	1.06	1.18	1.81	0.81
2020-25	1.01	1.20	1.71	0.81
2025-30	0.98	1.22	1.62	0.83
2030-35	0.99	1.25	1.56	0.86
2035-40	1.02	1.29	1.51	0.90
2040-45	1.05	1.33	1.47	0.94
2045-50	1.06	1.36	1.42	0.97

Source: UN.

Discussion and concluding remarks

Since the early sixties of last century an exponential growth of world population was assumed in many influential circles including the UN and most Western governmental circles.[18] Even most recently, after signs to the contrary are increasingly evident, respected media personalities (like Stephen Hawking) insist on the specter of exponential growth. It is straightforward to construct a Malthusian projection for 1985-2050 using $GR = 1.85$ percent that corresponds to the increase of world population between 1985-1990 by means of

$$P_{Malthus}\left(t\right)_{n+1} = P\left(t\right)_{n}\left(1+\left(GR\right)_{n}\right)^{t} \tag{3}$$

For 2010, the Malthusian projection gives a world population of 7.60×10^{9} — instead of the actual population of 6.90×10^{9} — and would continue growing exponentially.[19]

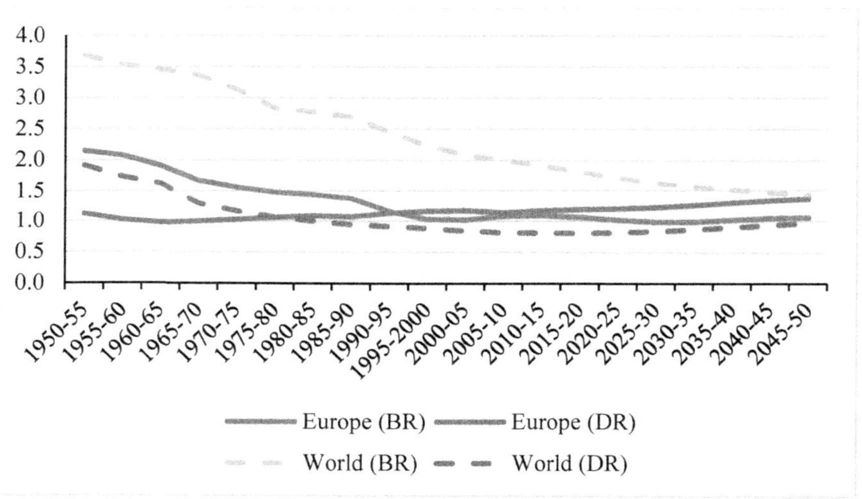

Figure 12.5. Birth rates (*BR*) and death rates (*DR*) for the World and Europe 1950-2050
Source: UN.

Table 12.3 (above) gives the numerical data for these projections. Figure 12.6 depicts these results for the period 1950-2010 (actual data) together with those of the Malthusian projection, the *IRE* projection and UN projection (low fertility variant, the more realistic) for (2010-2050).[20] Finally, Figure 12.7 compares *IRE* projections with the most recent UN's ones, for low, medium and high fertility scenarios.

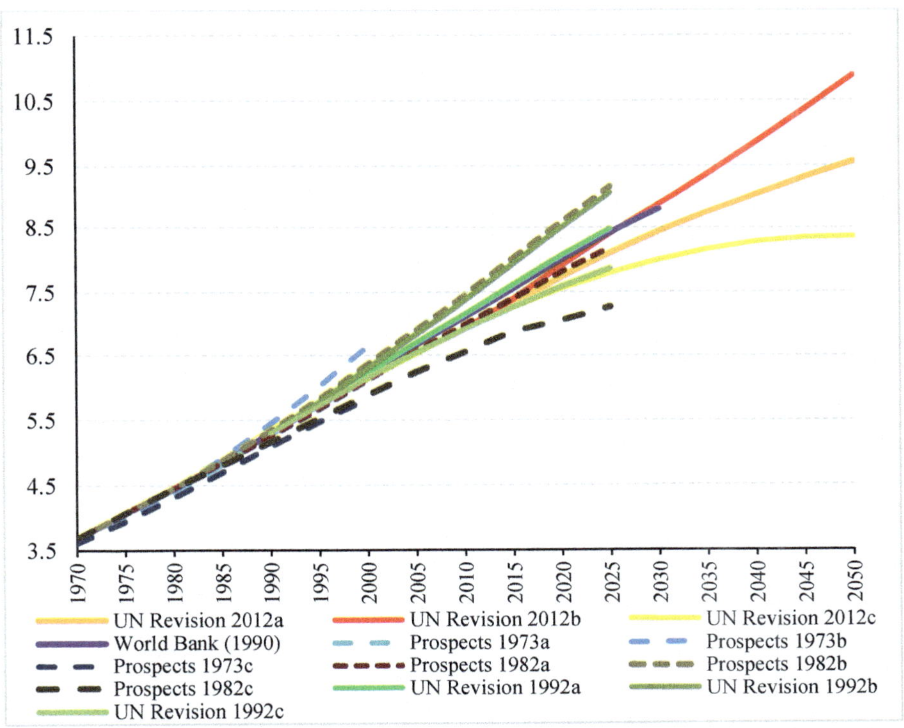

Figure 12.6a. UN world population projections 1950-2050. Note: The shadow area corresponds to projections.

Source: UN data and (IRE) model projection –Eq. (1). $1/2 \Delta P_m (\tanh \alpha) = 2.93$, $\tau = 32$, $t_{inf} = 1985$, $P_{RL} = 2.0$.

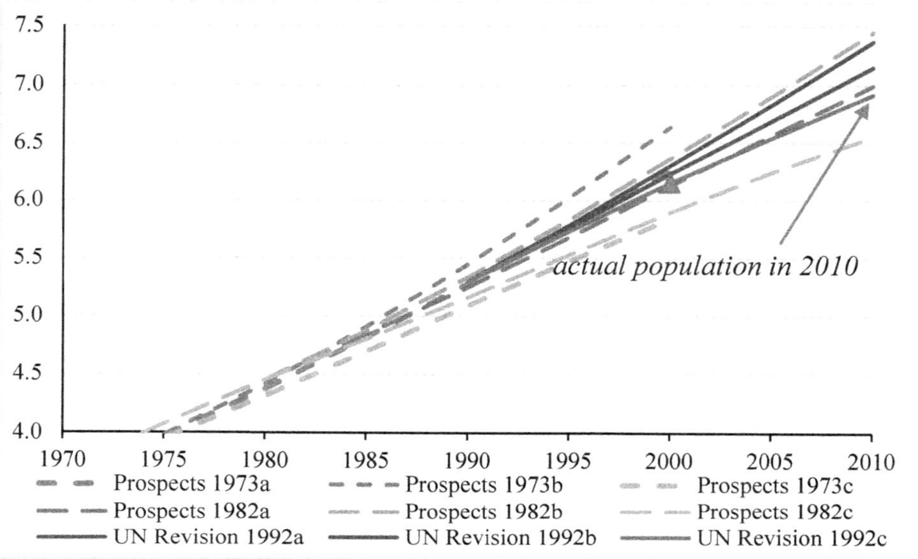

Figure 12.6b. UN world population 'over-estimation' of population growth 1950-2010

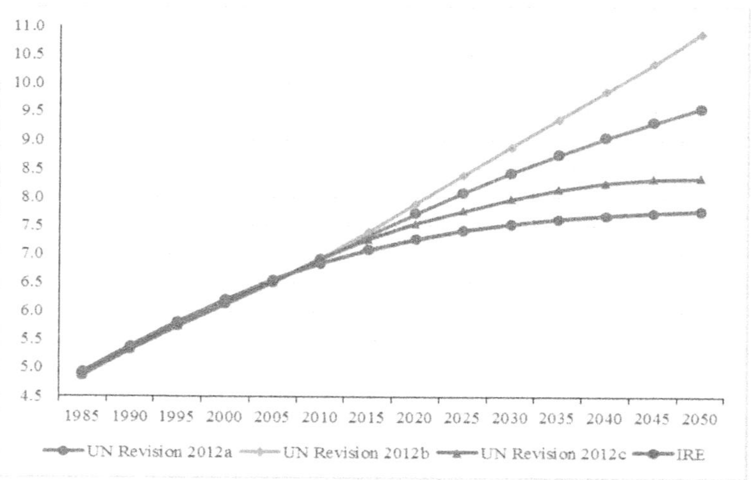

Figure 12.7. UN world population projections 1950-2050: A comparison between UN 2012 Rev. and *IRE* projections (pop. in billions)

Although the estimation given by the IRE method is significantly lower, experience shows (at least in the last decades) that the UN tends to systematically overestimate population growth, to the point that data show that the nearest scenario to what finally happens gets nearer to the low fertility variant than the medium and high variants (see Figure 6b).

The main findings and implications of our approach may be summarized as follows:

(1) A continuous exponential world population growth (Malthusian régime) is unrealistic. The exponential growth registered in the XX Century until approximately 1985 was mainly a consequence of an increase in life expectency (LE), with a constant decline in birth rates. Rather, steps up (alternated with relatively stable periods or step down) should be expected. Usually, an increase in life expectancy is followed by a gradual decrease in fertility rate. However, certain drastic policies promoting contraception and abortion (as is the case of China) may result in unwanted population trends with deleterious human, social and economic consequences.[21]

(2) It is interesting to note that the local population density in various countries with annual *per capita* income in the range 15,000 to 45,000 USD is between five times and fifteen times higher than the present average world population.[22] This suggests that, in any case, economic growth allows to maintain largest populations (Hayek, 1988; Simon, 1977).

(3) Taking into account that: (a) the replacement level fertility rate is about $FR=2.1$ child per woman; (b) the birth rate is of the order of $BR=(0.75)FR$; (c) the life expectancy at fertility age (about 18 years), $(LE_{fa})=(LE_b)-18$, and for cases like Europe and

Japan, for which population has leveled out already (and is even decreasing) as shown above, $(LE_b) \simeq (DR)/(0.833))$, population replacement level $(BR = DR)$ is attained when

$$BR = \left[(0.75) \times 2.1\right] \times 10^{-2} = 1.57 \times 10^{-2} = DR \tag{4}$$

corresponding to

$$(LE_b) = 18 + (DR)/(0.833) = 70.8 \text{ years} \tag{5}$$

An increase in women's life expectancy beyond 70.8 years is unlikely to result in an increase of birth rate.

(4) Additionally, graphs of population data of steps up in population for all continents could be fitted by means of *IRE* model (Eq. 1) for Africa, Europe, Asia, Northern America and Latin America. To this end, first the inflection point (corresponding to the maximum slope) for the step up in population should be estimated. This would allow us to get t_{inf}, $P(t_{\text{inf}})$, P_{RL}, and ΔP_m^* for each continent. Then τ^* is determined by means of

$$\tau^* = (\pm \Delta t)/\tanh^{-1}\left(\frac{2P(\pm \Delta t) - P_{RL}}{\Delta P_m^*}\right) \tag{6}$$

Where the data for $-\Delta t$ is well known, in principle, for all continents while data for $+\Delta t$ is not for Africa, Europe, Asia, Northern America, Latin America and Oceania. If data for $-\Delta t$ and $+\Delta t$ were available it is possible to calculate an average $\tau^* = \frac{1}{2}\left[\tau^*(-\Delta t) + \tau^*(+\Delta t)\right]$. If not, it is still possible to use $\tau^* \approx \tau^*(-\Delta t)$.

Finally, in this chapter we have focused in the *inertia* of the demographic evolution. Neither the effects of migrations over population size by continents (not a limitation because the world is a closed system) nor any demographic or economic hypothesis/explanation about the decision of reducing birth rates have been included. These decisions might be seen as limitations of our approach; however this is not the case. As has been said, our model captures the inertia of a system that is not going to change radically its trend within the time span considered. Think about the very fact that most of future mothers (2015-2050) are born. Of course, further investigation of world population trends and their implications from other points of view deserves special attention on their own.

REFERENCES

[1] Of course, there is more complex models in which population growth rate (n) is the result of households optimal decisions about how many children they desire, including a substitution effect in the case of households of more developed countries — the number of desired children is lower, the larger the level of per capita wealth (or income). See, for example Barro and Becker (1989); Becker (1976, 1981 [1991]).

[2] Data source: UN Population Division (http://www.un.org/esa/population/unpop.htm). For the years 1920, 1930, 1940 and 1950 the source is UN (1959) Demographic Yearbook, New York, p. 127.

[3] As the World Fertility Report 2013: Fertility at the Extremes (Nations, 2014) shows, 66 countries with more than 3.2 children per woman in 2005-2010 (45 out of 66 concentrated in sub-Saharan Africa) and 70 countries with 2.0 children per woman or less in 2005-2010.

[4] An excellent survey on mathematical population dynamics is Bacaër (2011). See also Miranda and Lima (2010; 2011). The IRE model (see Eq. 1 below) is an improvement over the simple rate equations solution given in Gonzalo, Muñoz, and Santos (2013, p.: 194).

[5] Applying the model to the world as a whole, has several advantages, the main one is that the world is a closed system (without net migrations) that 'preserves energy'.

[6] In other words, replacement level (RL) means that birth rates and death rates are equal at that instant of time.

[7] In human beings, the (recorded) 'maximum life span' is 122 years.

[8] The proportionality factors for each continent have been determined by means of a representative sample of the most populous countries in each continent.

[9] Along the paper we use this variant because is the most 'conservative' scenario. However, as will be shown, UN projections under low-fertility

variant has been historically more consistent with actual data as time went by (see Figure 6 below).

[10] For simplicity, in the rest of the paper we omit references to Oceania.

[11] Projections under UN 2012 Revision medium fertility variant. These umbers may seem quite exaggerate, due to the specific demographic dynamics projected for Latin America.

[12] Full details of this expression can be found in Gonzalo et al. (2013).

[13] In this case, we define

$$\tau^* = \tau / \tanh \alpha.$$

[14] According to UN data (1990-2010), Japan -a large rich and ageing country- shows a similar time reversal.

[15] More direct data for death rate and life expectancy might show perhaps a little less statistical scatter; however the general trend is clear.

[16] From 2010-2050 we represent UN projections for low-fertility variant.

[17] Even though migrations.

[18] The Club of Rome was the most famous and perhaps most influential one. See also the interest of Science on this topic: (Aldrich, 1968; Caldwell, 2008; Dorn, 1962; Holden, 1974, 1984; Horiuchi, 1992; Mead, 1974; Sachs, 2002; Sax, 1969).

[19] Assuming a growth rate of 1.85% and departing from actual population in 1985. See calculations in Table 3 above.

[20] It would be very interesting to analyze whether with pre-1965 pre-chemical contraceptives, pre-legalized abortion, and modest 'spontaneous' decrease in fertility rates, world population would have leveled out at mid-21st Century. However, this exercise is out of the scope of this paper.

[21] An example of this concern is a recent report urging a change in China's one child policy. See The Guardian, 31st October 2012, 'China think-tank urges end of one-child policy. Foundation close to central leadership urges end to birth limits policy across China by 2015, with

experts saying reform is 'inevitable'.' The cited think-tank is China Development Research Foundation (http://www.cdrf.org.cn/en/).

[22] For instance: in UK, 5 time larger; in the Netherlands, 8 times; in Puerto Rico, 9 times; in South Korea, 10 times; in Taiwan, 13 times. Not counting exceptional cases like Hong Kong (with 6.4 million inhabitants), 126 times and Singapore (with 7.0 million inhabitants) which has 139 times the world average.

CHAPTER 13

QUANTITATIVE ESTIMATES OF THE FUTURE
WORLD POPULATION DECLINE[*]

by Julio A. Gonzalo and Manuel Alfonseca

Introduction

As pointed out recently by Michael J. Kelly[1] a collapse of global civilization as predicted by Ehrlich[2] is unrealistic because a balanced assessment of the historical progress being made suggests otherwise. In his words:

> *The population explosion (and its Malthusian societal disruptions) that Ehrlich FRS predicted for the 1990s has not come about..., and the concerns in this present Ehrlich paper are not tempered by the mounting evidence of the demographic transition that occurs when the majority of people live in cities and have access to education. In Japan, Europe and North America the population, excluding immigration, is in decline. Some studies indicate that a peak of 9 billion people in 2050 will be followed by a decline to a population of approximately 6 billion in 2100—less than that in 2000... and bringing new problems of unwanted infrastructure assets! The UN is revising its future population estimates downward.... If we look at the waste in the contemporary food chain, at the point of growth, in transit to the*

---

[*] Gonzalo, J.A., Alfonseca, M., 2015. *Quantitative estimates of the future world population decline.* Journal of Global Issues and Solutions, The Bimonthly Journal of the BWW Society, 6 pp.

market and into the homes of consumers, and compound that loss by the amount of food thrown out rather than consumed, we generate the quantity of food to feed the 9 billion today with the systems in place if we were less wasteful and could distribute it...

Previous work[3] investigated claims (Science, 4 Nov. 1960) that world population would approach infinity in the third decade of the 21st century. On the other hand, a plot of world population (1960-2010) as given by the UN shows clearly that it will approach a maximum about the year 2050, and then will start going down.

Improved solutions to the two complex rate equations describing world population trends have been shown to describe it well from 1950 to 2010 and can be used to estimate it reasonably beyond 2010. As global birth rate (BR) has decreased consistently in those years, a continued exponential growth of world population is certainly not realistic. Current population growth must be entirely due to global increase in life expectancy, i.e. the decrease in death rate (DR). This increase, which has been documented since the middle of the twentieth century, should not be expected to proceed beyond 85 years, as current data show for Europe and the U.S. In fact, the death rate has been growing in Europe and Japan for over a decade, due to the aging of the population.

As shown below, a large step-up in population, as what took place during the last century, can be characterized by a significant decrease followed by a subsequent decrease in birth rate. This was evident in the early fifties, before antinatalist policies became recommended or enforced by the UN and the governments of the leading countries in Europe, America and Asia. International groups like *Planned Parenthood* have carried out effective antinatalist campaigns, intensifying abnormally the natural decrease in birth rate already under way, so that we are now facing a possible population decrease after 2050 with unwonted consequences.

A population step-up, followed by a subsequent step-down is in principle describable with the same kind of rate equations used previously (1) to describe an isolated step-up.

Around 1900, the death and birth rates were BR≈DR≈40×10^{-3}, leading to a stable population level.

Population step down

In ordinary circumstances, a population step-up is driven by an increase in life expectancy, followed (after a certain delay) by a decrease in birth rate. The characteristic time (τ) is computed as the inverse of the square root of DR and BR, resulting, after the transient, in a new replacement level at a higher population. The analogous process of a population step-down also begins by an increase in death rate (which of course could, but should not be artificially induced) followed eventually, after a certain delay, by an increase in birth rate until a new stable level is reached. The longer the birth rate delay, the more serious the succeeding population decrease.

Our planet is a closed system, in the sense that we do not expect aliens to come to us as immigrants, or a massive migration of Earth people to far away planets. The total sustainable human population on Earth has been estimated[2] as one order of magnitude larger than the current 7 billion population.

Data analysis

Table 13.1 shows the world population UN data, where the three values in the world DR and BR columns after 2010 are projections corresponding to three different birth rate scenarios: low, medium and high fertility. It can be observed that both death rate (DR) and inverse life expectancy (LE^{-1}) have decreased simultaneously between 1950 and 2010. Table 13.2 shows the data for different parts of the world, where only the low fertility scenario is shown.

Table 13.3 shows some computations on the DR/BR values, extended to 2050 using the low fertility scenario. The two computed values are the following:

$$\alpha = 0.5\ln(BR/DR) \qquad \tau = 500/\sqrt{BR.DR}$$

Table 13.1. UN 2012 data for the world
(http://esa.un.org/wpp/Demographic-Profiles/index.shtm)

Dates			World				
	GR	DR		BR			LE
1950-55	1.79	19.1		37.0			47
1955-60	1.83	17.3		35.6			49
1960-65	1.91	16.2		35.3			51
1965-70	2.07	12.9		33.5			57
1970-75	1.96	11.6		31.1			59
1975-80	1.78	10.6		28.3			61
1980-85	1.78	10.0		27.8			62
1985-90	1.80	9.4		27.4			64
1990-95	1.52	9.1		24.3			65
1995-00	1.30	8.8		21.8			66
2000-05	1.22	8.4		20.6			67
2005-10	1.20	8.1		20.1			69
2010-15	0.96	8.1	8.1	8.0	21.4	19.5	17.7	70

Table 13.1. (Cont'd)

Dates	World							
	GR	DR			BR			LE
2015-20	0.76	8.0	8.1	8.1	21.2	18.5	15.7	71
2020-25	0.60	8.0	8.1	8.3	20.4	17.4	14.3	72
2025-30	0.51	8.1	8.3	8.6	19.3	16.6	13.7	73
2030-35	0.41	8.3	8.6	9.1	18.7	16.1	13.2	74
2035-40	0.29	8.5	9.0	9.6	18.6	15.6	12.5	74
2040-45	0.17	8.7	9.4	10.2	18.6	15.2	11.8	75
2045-50	0.04	8.8	9.7	10.8	18.5	14.8	11.2	76
2050-55	-0.07	8.8	9.9	11.3	18.2	14.4	10.7	77

Table 13.2. UN 2012 data for parts of the world
(http://esa.un.org/wpp/Demographic-Profiles/index.shtm)

Dates	Europe		Asia		N.America		L. America		Africa	
	DR	BR	DR	BR	DR	BR	DR	BR	DR	BR
1950-55	11.2	21.5	22.6	42.0	9.5	24.6	15.5	42.6	26.8	48.1
1955-60	10.2	20.9	20.2	39.5	9.3	24.8	13.7	41.8	24.3	47.9
1960-65	9.7	19.0	18.9	39.7	9.3	22.5	12.2	41.0	22.2	47.4
1965-70	9.9	16.8	13.3	37.9	9.4	18.1	10.9	37.8	20.4	46.4
1970-75	10.2	15.6	11.3	34.3	9.2	15.6	9.7	35.2	18.7	45.9

Table 13.2. (Cont'd)

Dates	Europe		Asia		N.America		L. America		Africa	
	DR	BR	DR	BR	DR	BR	DR	BR	DR	BR
1975-80	10.5	14.8	9.9	29.7	8.6	14.9	8.7	33.0	17.1	45.5
1980-85	10.8	14.4	9.1	28.9	8.5	15.4	7.8	30.7	15.7	44.4
1985-90	10.6	13.7	8.5	28.7	8.6	15.7	7.1	27.9	14.6	42.6
1990-95	11.2	11.5	8.0	24.5	8.5	15.4	6.5	25.4	14.4	40.4
1995-00	11.5	10.2	7.6	21.0	8.5	14.2	6.1	23.6	13.8	38.8
2000-05	11.6	10.1	7.1	19.3	8.4	13.8	6.0	21.6	13.2	37.7
2005-10	11.3	10.8	7.0	18.5	8.1	13.7	5.9	19.3	11.8	36.7
2010-15	11.7	9.1	7.1	15.8	8.2	11.4	5.9	16.0	10.4	33.7
2015-20	12.0	8.1	7.3	13.5	8.4	10.4	6.1	13.8	9.5	30.9
2020-25	12.3	7.2	7.7	11.8	8.7	9.8	6.3	12.1	8.8	28.6
2025-30	12.7	7.1	8.3	11.1	9.2	9.8	6.7	11.3	8.3	27.3
2030-35	13.3	7.2	9.1	10.4	9.8	9.6	7.2	10.3	7.9	25.8
2035-40	14	7.2	10.0	9.6	10.5	9.4	7.8	9.4	7.6	24.2
2040-45	15	7.0	10.9	8.9	11.1	9.1	8.6	8.4	7.4	22.4
2045-50	15	6.6	11.9	8.2	11.5	8.7	9.4	7.7	7.3	20.8
2050-55	16	6.4	12.8	7.7	11.7	8.4	10.3	7.2	7.3	19.4

Table 13.3. Some computations on the smoothed UN data

Dates	DR	BR	x=BR/DR	y=BR*DR	α	τ
1950-55	19.1	37	1.94	706.7	0.33	18.81
1955-60	17.3	35.6	2.06	615.9	0.36	20.15
1960-65	16.2	35.3	2.18	571.9	0.39	20.91
1965-70	12.9	33.5	2.60	432.2	0.48	24.05
1970-75	11.6	31.1	2.68	360.8	0.49	26.32
1975-80	10.6	28.3	2.67	300.0	0.49	28.87
1980-85	10	27.8	2.78	278.0	0.51	29.99
1985-90	9.4	27.4	2.91	257.6	0.53	31.16
1990-95	9.1	24.3	2.67	221.1	0.49	33.62
1995-00	8.8	21.8	2.48	191.8	0.45	36.10
2000-05	8.4	20.6	2.45	173.0	0.45	38.01
2005-10	8.1	20.1	2.48	162.8	0.45	39.19
2010-15	8	17.7	2.21	141.6	0.40	42.02
2015-20	8.1	15.7	1.94	127.2	0.33	44.34
2020-25	8.3	14.3	1.72	118.7	0.27	45.89
2025-30	8.6	13.7	1.59	117.8	0.23	46.06
2030-35	9.1	13.2	1.45	120.1	0.19	45.62
2035-40	9.6	12.5	1.30	120.0	0.13	45.64
2040-45	10.2	11.8	1.16	120.4	0.07	45.58
2045-50	10.8	11.2	1.04	121.0	0.02	45.46
2050-55	11.3	10.7	0.95	120.9	-0.03	45.47

Figure 13.1 plots the death rate (DR) for the world (1960-2010) as a function of inverse life expectancy (1950-2000). It can be seen that DR seems to be approaching a minimum and is clearly on the rise in Europe. This is an inevitable consequence of the fact that older generations are approaching their maximum life expectancy.

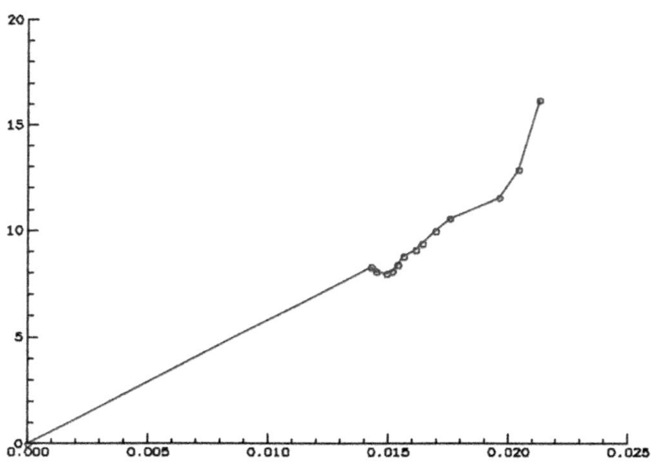

Figure 13.1. DR vs LE^{-1} (DR delayed by 10 years)

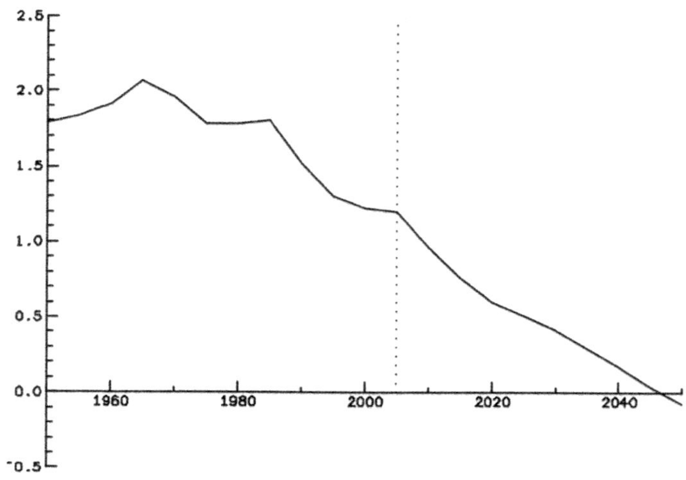

Figure 13.2. Growth rate vs time for the low fertility scenario. Prediction begins at the right of the dashed vertical line (the 2005-2010 interval)

Figure 13.2 shows world population growth rate (GR) for the lower fertility scenario. Figures before 1950 are scattered and unreliable, but they show that GR was significantly smaller than 1% by 1900.

Figures 13.3 to 13.5 illustrate the population step-up as a function of time for the three different future scenarios. Figure 13.3 shows how the population step-up takes place through a pronounced decrease in DR followed, after some delay, by a similar decrease in BR. Figure 13.3a shows the low fertility scenario, where DR≈BR by 2050-2055, a time at which a population step-down could start to take over (see Figure 13.2). Figure 13.3b shows the same information for the medium fertility scenario, where this effect would be delayed by about 50 years.

Figure 13.4 shows α as a function of time for the three UN scenarios. It can be seen that a maximum was reached around 1985 (the population inflection point). The average of this variable between 1950 and 2010 is 2.48. For the low fertility scenario, x becomes 1 around 2050 and its decrease after 1985 is more pronounced than its increase before that date.

Figure 13.5 represents the characteristic time (τ) in the same conditions. Its value goes up quite linearly from about 19 years by 1950 to about 40 years by 2010, but is supposed to stop growing by 2005-2010 in the high fertility scenario, and by 2020 in the medium and low scenarios.

Figure 13.6 shows the birth and death rates for the world and Europe between 1950 and 2010, together with extrapolated values for the world according to the three alternative scenarios. For the low fertility scenario, the crossing of death and birth rates is to be expected by 2050, and the expected average of x=BR/DR between 2050 and 2100 would be between 0.75 and 0.85, implying a substantial decrease for the world population around 2010.

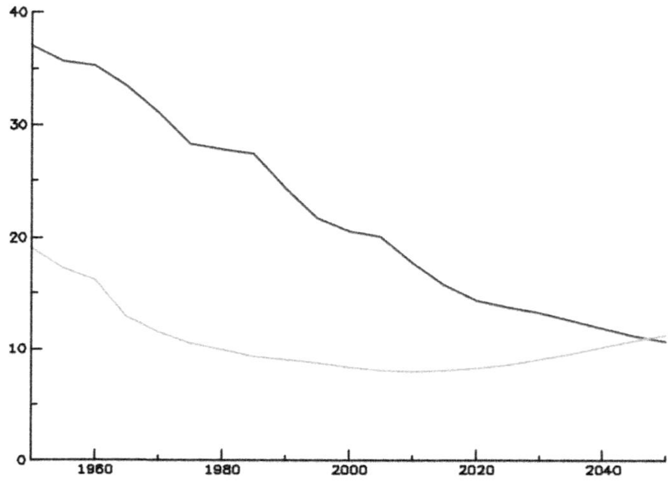

Figure 13.3a. DR and BR vs time for the low fertility scenario. Top: BR; bottom: DR

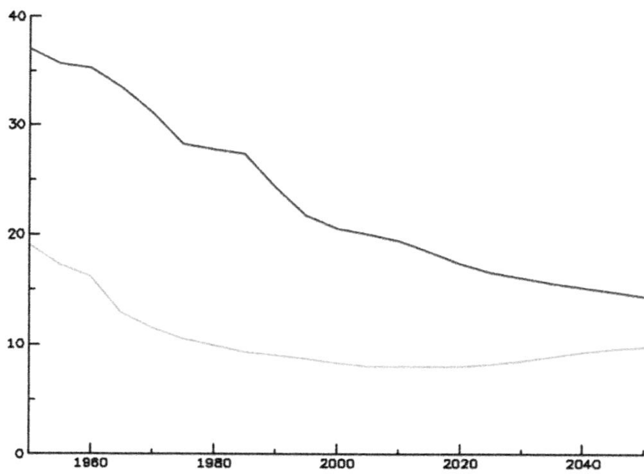

Figure 13.3b. DR and BR vs time for the medium fertility scenario. Top: BR; bottom: DR

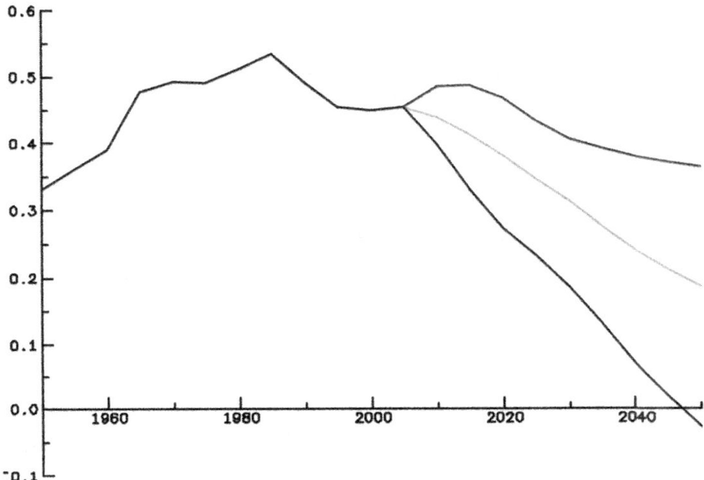

Figure 13.4. α vs time for the three future scenarios. Bottom: lower fertility; middle: medium fertility; top: high fertility

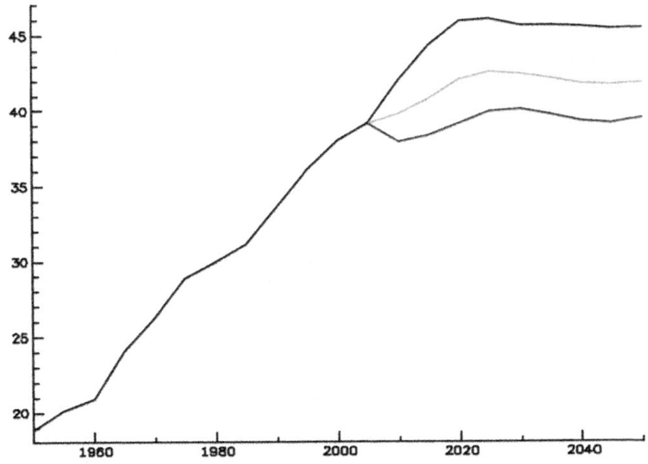

Figure 13.5. τ vs time for the three future scenarios. Top: lower fertility; medium: medium fertility; bottom: high fertility

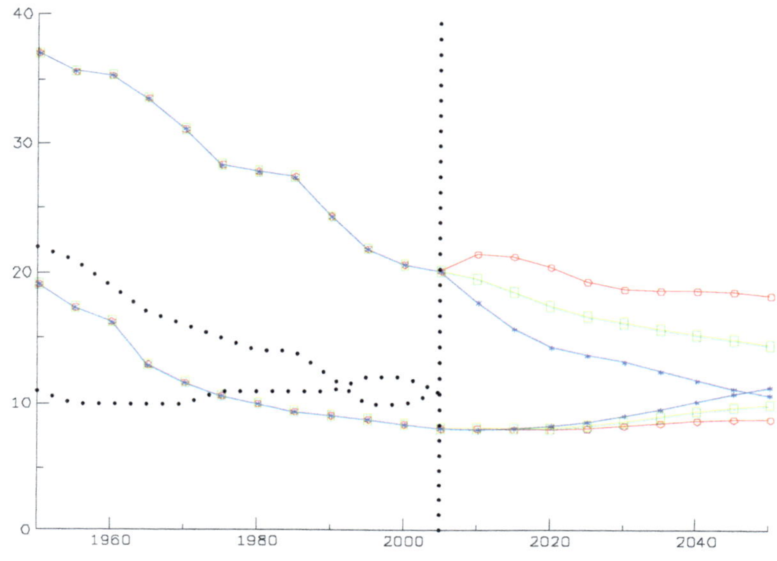

Figure 13.6. DR and BR vs time for the World and Europe. Dashed lines: Europe. Full lines: World. Blue: lower fertility; green: medium fertility; red: high fertility. Predictions begin at the right of the dashed vertical line (the 2005-2010 interval)

During the step-up, the world population can be represented[1] by the following equation:

$$P(t) = P_{RL} + \frac{1}{2} [\Delta P_{max} \tanh \alpha][1 + \tanh \frac{t-t_i}{\tau_i}] \qquad (1)$$

where $P_{RL} \approx 2 \times 10^9$ (replacement level of the world population around 1900), $\frac{1}{2} [\Delta P_{max} \tanh \alpha] \approx 2.9 \times 10^9$, $t_i = 1985$ (inflection time), and $\tau_i = 33$ years, resulting in $P_{max} = P(2050) = 7.7 \times 10^9$.

During the step-down, we will consider two cases: x=BR/DR=0.85 and x=0.75. The appropriate equation for the step down would be:

$$P(t) = P_{max} + \frac{1}{2} [\Delta P_{max} \tanh \alpha][1 + \tanh \frac{t-t_i}{\tau_i}] \qquad (2)$$

where $P_{max} \approx 7.7 \times 10^9$ (world population around 2050), $\frac{1}{2} [\Delta P_{max} \tanh \alpha] \approx 0.314 \times 10^9$, $t_i = 2050 + 33$ (estimated inflection time for the step down), and $\tau \approx 33$ years, for $\bar{x} = 0.85$; or $\frac{1}{2} [\Delta P_{max} \tanh \alpha] \approx 0.55 \times 10^9$ for $\bar{x} = 0.75$. This implies substantial world population decreases of almost half a billion (460 million) and about twice that (810 million) by 2100, respectively.

We can now estimate, using Figures 13.3–13.5, what would have been the step-up in population in the interval 1950-2010 if a natural decrease in birth rate would have been allowed, i.e. a continuation of the birth rate decrease which had been taking place during the sixties and early seventies, before drastic antinatalistic policies (chemical contraceptives, induced abortions, amoral sexual education and the like), supported by international pressure groups such as the UN, Planned Parenthood and the governments of the leading countries in Europe, America and Asia, had a substantial impact on world population trends. Introducing the pertinent changes in equation (1), we get Table 13.4.

Table 13.4. Comparison of the effect of antinatalistic policies

	$\langle x \rangle$	α	t_i	$[\Delta P_{max} \tanh \alpha]/2$	P_{max}
Actual step-up	2.15	0.382	1985	2.9×10^9	7.7×10^9
Natural step-up	2.30	0.416	1990	3.2×10^9	8.4×10^9

Conclusions

We can reach the following conclusions:

The exponential growth in world population assumed for years by the UN and the leading countries of the world is unrealistic.

Human population trends should not be manipulated under the false assumption that antinatalistic ideologues know better.

Today the world is not overpopulated and is unlikely to be so in the foreseeable future. In Asia, the most populated continent, many countries (Taiwan, South Korea, Japan, Hong Kong, Singapore...) have reached several times the average Gross National Income for the world.

Extrapolating present trends shows that total world population may reach a maximum of 7.74 billion by 2050, and by the end of the current century it may have decreased by half a billion to a billion.

Assuming that the relatively smooth natural decrease in birth rate underway by the mid-seventies had continued all the way towards a new replacement level, the estimated population maximum would have reached 8.4 billion by 2065, rather than 7.73 billion by 2050, and the now expected step-down by 2100 could have been avoided. Therefore the antinatalistic policies supported by the UN should be reconsidered.

The population rising during this century (1950-2050) is due to the high and sustained decrease in death rate (and the corresponding high increase in life expectation) rather than an increase in fertility that actually never happened.

REFERENCES

[1] Kelly, M.J., 2013. *Why a collapse of global civilization will be avoided: a comment on Ehrlich & Ehrlich*, Proc. R. Soc., V.282, I.1802, DOI:10.1098/rspb.2013.1193.

[2] Ehrlich, P.R., Ehrlich, A., 2013. *Can a collapse of global civilization be avoided?* Proc. R. Soc. B 280, 20122845, DOI:10.1098/rspb.2012.2845.

[3] Gonzalo, J.A., Muñoz, F.F., 2014. *Prospects of world population decline in the near future: a short note.* Departamento de Análisis Económico, U.A.M.

[4] Gonzalo, J.A., Muñoz, F.F., F.F., Santos, D.J., 2012. *Using a rate equation approach to model world population trends.* Simulation 89(2), 192-198, DOI:10.1177/0037549712463736.

CHAPTER 14
MALTHUS'S MISTAKE
by Manuel Alfonseca and Julio A. Gonzalo

Since the end of the eighteenth century, apocalyptic warnings as regards the unstoppable increase of the world population have followed one another. In 1798, Thomas Robert Malthus published *An essay on the principle of population, as it affects the future improvement of society, with remarks on the speculations of Mr. Godwin, M. Condorcet, and other writers*. This essay includes the famous quotation:

Assuming then my postulata as granted, I say, that the power of population is indefinitely greater than the power in the earth to produce subsistence for man.

Population, when unchecked, increases in a geometrical ratio. Subsistence increases only in an arithmetical ratio. A slight acquaintance with numbers will shew the immensity of the first power in comparison of the second.

In 1838, as a reaction against Malthus and his alarmism, Pierre François Verhoult asserted in his *Note on the law of population growth* that this growth is not a geometric progression, but follows a *logistic curve* (see Figure 14.1). This curve appears frequently in many natural growth processes.

In spite of this, the first report of the Club of Rome (*The limits of growth*, 1974) insisted again on an alarmist position by keeping to the previsions of Malthus (an exponential growth) without taking into account the study by Verhoult. In this context, several political and social movements have presented contraceptives and abortion as inevitable measures to save humanity from the disaster of overpopulation.

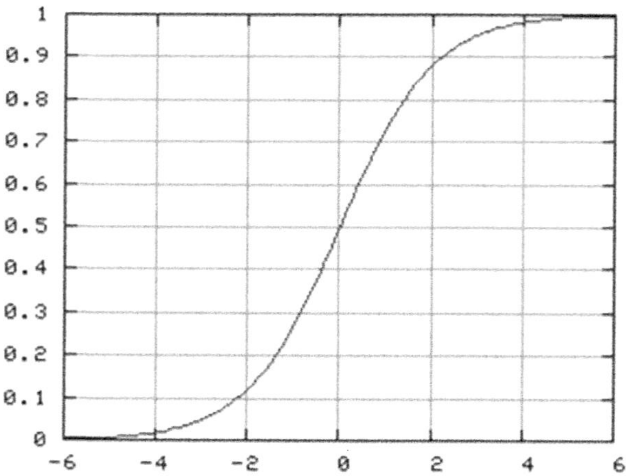

Figure 14.1. The logistic curve for K=1

However, current forecasts are very different. In 2012 the UN published its data about the growth of the world population from 1950-2010, which showed that the growth rate has declined, and that the turning point of the curve (which is looking more and more like the logistic curve) was gone through around 1985. Based on these data, the UN have made several estimates of the future growth of the world population, the most optimistic of which predicts that a maximum of some 8300 million people will be reached by 2050.

Based on these data, and other less detailed covering the period between 1900 and 1950, the authors of this post have approximated the real growth of the world population and its extrapolation till 2050 by the following mathematical expression:

$$\frac{dp(t)}{dt} = \frac{1}{\tau}\left[\sinh\alpha - p(\mathrm{t})\cosh\alpha\right]$$

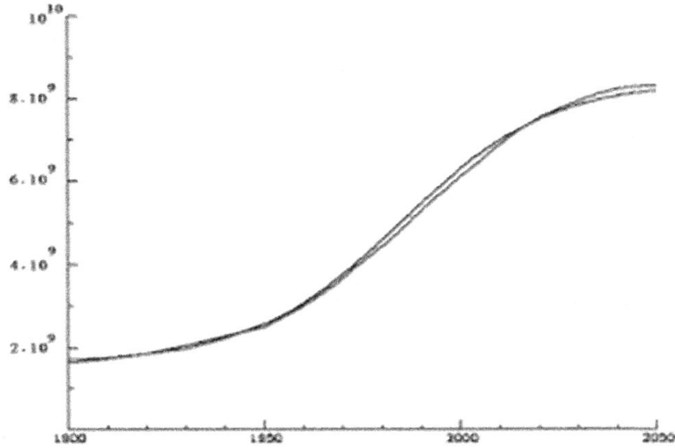

Figure 14.2. Comparison of UN data (real and predicted) with those generated by the previous equation

Figure 14.2 compares the UN data (real and predicted) with those generated by the previous equation. Next we have estimated the development of the world population if anti-natalist policies had not been implemented around the seventies. We have obtained the following results: the turning point would have been delayed until 1990, just five years later. And by 2075 the population would have reached a maximum of 9 billion: 700 million more people, about twenty five years later.

The inevitable conclusion is that anti-natalist policies do not give the expected results. This is now so obvious in China, that it has led them to put an end to their one-child policy. The hundreds of millions of children sacrificed on the altar to Moloch have not been killed to save humanity, but so that we can share a little more for a little longer. It won't be surprising if posterity accuses us of barbarism for allowing abortion against all scientific evidence, just as we accuse our ancestors for allowing slavery.

AUTHOR INDEX

CPSIA information can be obtained
at www.ICGtesting.com
Printed in the USA
BVOW10*0657110716

454672BV00004B/1/P